LIFE IN THE RENAISSANCE

A Chanticleer Press Edition

LIFE IN THE

RENAISSANCE

MARZIEH GAIL

Illustrated
with many old prints
paintings and carvings

A Landmark Giant

RANDOM HOUSE

 BY RANDOM HOUSE, INC.

All rights reserved under International and Pan-American Copyright Conventions.
Published in New York by Random House, Inc.
Distributed in Canada by Random House of Canada Limited, Toronto.

PLANNED AND PRODUCED BY CHANTICLEER PRESS, NEW YORK

Library of Congress Catalog Card Number 68-29585
Printed by Amilcare Pizzi, S.p.A., Milano, Italy

CONTENTS

I Panorama of an Age

If we could travel back in time and see outspread before us a panorama of the Renaissance, we would surely be drawn first to the great cities of Italy—Venice, Florence, Rome, Siena, Padua, Bologna, Verona. For there the glories of ancient Rome and Greece seemed to be reborn.

Passing through the towered gates and into one of these cities we move down crowded streets. Many are still as narrow and crooked as they had been in the Middle Ages but some are now paved and are being widened, and there are more palatial mansions. On most streets the houses stand one against the other, with tiled roofs and doorlike unglassed windows with bars at the street level. Mules, heavily laden, serve for trucks, as do the dray horses pulling a haywagon; and there are donkeys for taxis. A man is herding goats through the streets. An old woman in a white kerchief cradles a goose in her arms and tries to avoid a stray dog. A woman in a third-floor window draws up a bundle on a rope by means of a pulley attached to the wall above her head. Craftsmen work in shops open to the street; some of their wares are displayed on a counter out front. In a church, a bishop with an ornamented miter on his head preaches to kneeling worshippers. Farther along, in a cell-like room, a teacher instructs his pupils, who sit listening, chin on hand.

On a river in the foreground we see a picnic party, men and women in an open, canopied boat, with a wineflask hanging over the side to cool. Through one of the city gates, lords and ladies mounted on spirited horses are trotting out to the hunt. A noble in a knee-length garment has a hunting hawk perched on his wrist. The ladies wear big hats and long skirts. A page, with one leg of his tights striped red and the other leg black and white, leads a greyhound on a leash.

The lovely countryside spreads out before them, empty except for a thatched cottage or two. Oxen go plodding past. Peasants scratch with their mattocks at the ground; one is holding part of a statue he has dug up. A figure standing motionless in a field, drawing his bow and about to shoot an arrow, is only a scarecrow.

Moving to another city, we see brick houses, their tall open windows crowded with fine ladies who are watching knights in armor staging mock battles, galloping great battle horse against battle horse, breaking lance against lance. Behind a fence, little boys

Travelers look for lodgings at public inns in Florence.

6

in caps and knee-length coats and tights watch the pageantry from the tops of tables or stools or by looking through knotholes. In the center of a square is a bronze statue of Perseus grasping a severed head. In another part of the square is a gallows with a hanged man swinging from it.

A glimpse into the studio of an artist shows him sitting at an easel, looking through a measuring instrument at his model, a young girl in draperies strewn with flowers. Outside, a leper, rattling a wooden clapper to warn passersby of his presence, shuffles past, a large purse at his belt. High in a niche is a statue of the Madonna and Child. A pilgrim wearing on his hat a collection of leaden badges from the shrines he has visited, rides by on a tired palfrey. In a high-ceilinged room, students are gathered around a table on which a dead man is stretched out. A surgeon with a knife stands over the corpse; from a platform above, a professor tells him how to dissect the body.

In another city we see a bridal procession, obviously of the nobility, winding through the streets. Following some archers are trumpeters,

Below left:
Boating and riding were common pastimes of young nobles.
Below right:
A lord and lady ride to the hunt. Velvet, fringe and fur were correct hunting attire in the early sixteenth century.

Busy market stalls in southern France.

pipers and drummers, perhaps two hundred musicians in all. Then come long-robed bishops, ambassadors in black and gold, wearing gold chains and jeweled plumes, followed by a jester, and grooms in purple who lead the bride's dappled gray horse with its gold trappings. Then comes the bride herself on a roan mule, a mule curried, perhaps even rubbed with perfume and wearing a harness covered with roses of fine gold. The bride has yellow hair, gleaming and strung with rubies and pearls, and wears a dress of gold brocade. Four robed men, walking two to each side, hold up a canopy over her head. At the wedding party a fountain spurts wine, children sing and, near by, a rope-walker balances high above the cathedral square. Men and women guests stroll together, all in enormous headgear, the women shod in pattens several inches high and trailing long trains, the men in many-colored tights and knee-length brocades. A servant in black balances on his head a great serving dish of gold; musicians sit on a ledge covered with an oriental carpet and blare on trumpets.

Here is still another city with a domed cathedral like vertical sections of a peeled orange, and a tall bell tower. At a counter opening

on the street a man sorts piles of coins. Another shop displays a
variety of books; customers wearing spectacles browse leisurely
among the books.

Moving on we come upon a massive, columned villa, mirrored
in a canal. It has no outer walls. Near it is an elaborate box-
hedge maze. Farther along there is an open pavilion, like a band-
stand, where richly-dressed men and women sit banqueting at a
table that has a white cloth with a green border. Next is a city
with canals for streets. Here, at a corner, young toughs in jackets

*A horse race in the narrow
streets of Florence was full
of danger for jockeys,
horses and spectators.*

above their hips, colored tights and pointed shoes, are striking a cowering victim with their swords. An open doorway shows quite another scene: an old man sits in bed. Beside him a priest is praying. Farther along, through an upper window, we see two ladies playing chess. Standing beside them is a man with a greyhound on a leash.

In another place we see a cluster of tall, pastel-colored houses with narrow windows. Laundry flutters from a roof. Rising skyward are trumpet-like chimneys. On a balcony a priest holds up a cross,

while before him kneels a man, writhing and moaning, possessed of a devil, which the cross will draw out of him. In the street below, grave and confident and sure of their worth, robed businessmen converse. Farther on we come to a harbor and hundreds of ships with curved, high prows and sterns, tall sails and a crow's nest. Some of the ships have a row of cannon lining the lower deck.

Elsewhere, in a brick-walled garden, lovers embrace. A fountain is playing. A youth plucks a lute. Another holds a bottle of wine in a wicker container. Others are singing from a long scroll of music, four blow on trumpets, and one beats a drum. Through a gate we see streets paved in a checkerboard mosaic of black and white.

To the north, in Germany or Flanders, we see somber men in black, with collars of dark fur, walking past, some of them with Bible in hand. Outside the cities we come upon sturdy-looking peasants in coarse clothing, both the men and women with purses and knives at their belts. It is festival time and they dance and carouse.

Beggars, a common sight, held out their begging bowls for alms.

Impressions of the Renaissance

We come away from these scenes with three main impressions— the central themes of Renaissance life. Our first impression is that the Renaissance was a rediscovery of the great civilizations of the past, of ancient Greece and Rome. Literally meaning "rebirth," the Renaissance was a revival of interest in learning and in life. In order to go forward men had first to go back and study the great works of the past. In their search for knowledge and inspiration, scholars hunted out long-forgotten manuscripts and breathed new life into them. Sculptors dug up old statues out of the ground and once again admired the human body. Religious men returned to the Scriptures in old tongues. Explorers, suddenly free to explore this world after the medieval emphasis on the world of the spirit, pored over old maps and the writings of old travelers.

The second impression is that during the Renaissance the spotlight was on Italy, perhaps because Italy contained the heritage of ancient Rome. People turned to Italy, entertained Italians, copied Italian things. Beginning in the fourteenth century and continuing into the sixteenth, France, northern Europe and England often followed where Italy led.

The third impression is that in many ways the Renaissance was a spectacle, something to see, often dazzling. Patrons maintained

Overleaf:
Everybody marched in or watched religious festivals in Siena. The snail, elephant or unicorn on a float was a district emblem.

A farm woman collects a hog's blood for black pudding.

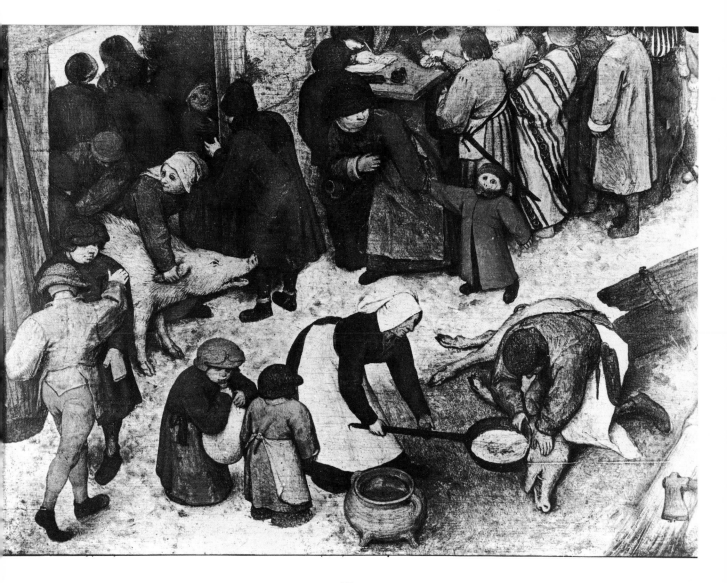

13

artists to immortalize them by painting them in all their magnificence, including their great chapels and palaces and ships; their horses, pets and servants; their glistening jewels, great balloon sleeves and stiff brocades. At no other period in history has western man gone so splendidly dressed.

Frederick III of Austria is crowned by the Pope at Rome.

Was the Renaissance world so different from the Middle Ages? Yes and no. In the Middle Ages each man—whether lord, craftsman or serf—had been born into his position and would live and die in it. But as trade increased and cities grew and education spread, occupations became more varied, and a man had a better chance to rise in life. Although religion was still a great force, men thought less of the spiritual world, of life after death, of heaven and hell, and more of this life and of worldly things—clothes, houses, pleasures. Man began to think of himself as an individual, who, although created by God, was himself capable of creating beauty—in buildings, paintings, statuary, jewelry. He began to explore the world around him, to create sciences that would help him understand the earth, the skies and his own body.

Chivalry was dying, the last medieval troubadour was dead, and the fanaticism of the Crusades was gone. Guns and bullets were replacing bows and arrows. The common man was being freed from

serfdom. Books were pouring from the newly-invented printing presses. European man was awakening as if from a long sleep. That is why many historians see the Renaissance as the beginning of our modern age.

2 A Renaissance City

Everyone agreed that Venice was the most enchanting of cities. She was so beautiful that the Venetians built a ramp to the top of her highest tower, so that horsemen could ride up and admire the view. For centuries this city was the great link between East and West. Merchants, crusaders and pilgrims came and went through her port and traveled in her ships. People of all races and faiths met, mingled and transacted business along her canals.

Turning away from the land, Venice seemed to float upon the sea. Actually, her houses rested on pilings, logs sunk into the layers of mud, sand and clay which make up the marshy islands within her great lagoon. To support her huge bell tower, workmen dug down through the wet ground till they reached firmer subsoil, and there they laid platforms of larch wood. As the years passed, these platforms and the pilings sank deeper and deeper, and had to be continually raised. Between the Renaissance and our own day, the buildings of Venice have been raised well over three feet.

A City Marries the Sea

So important was the sea to Venice that every spring there was a ritual in which the city "married" the Adriatic. The "wedding ceremony" was performed by the Doge or President of the Venetian Republic. At the head of a dazzling aquatic pageant, the Doge swept over the sheltered lagoon in his Bucentaur, a glittering state barge of gold and scarlet, until he came to the open sea. With him on the canopied deck, or following behind in gondolas shining with gold, were the real rulers of Venice, the Council of Ten and the Senate, besides nobles and ambassadors from other lands. The sweating oarsmen toiling away between decks provided a sharp contrast to all this glory, but even they had been outfitted in red or gold. Other barks and gondolas abrim with gentlemen and ladies in gorgeous dress accompanied the Bucentaur in such numbers that the water could hardly be seen. As the barge reached the open Adriatic, out beyond the barrier island of the Lido, the Doge rose from his throne. Solemnly to the green expanse of water he uttered the magic words: "O Sea, we wed thee, in token of our true dominion, which will never pass away." Then he tossed out the gold ring of marriage into the unanswering depths of the sea.

An everyday scene beside the Rialto drawbridge in Venice.

Boats were heeled over, like the one on the right, to repair leaking seams.

Venice lived from ships. Those "frogs of the marshes," the Venetians, had seen that their opportunities lay along the broad but dangerous highway of the sea. Though they adhered to the forms of the Catholic faith more closely than many Italians, and were excessively fond of holy relics, the Venetians never let religion stand in the way of trade. Other Christians might hate the Saracens, followers of the Prophet Muhammad; the Venetians did business with them. As well as cloth, iron and ship timbers, the Venetians sold Christian slaves to the Saracens, and weapons that could be turned against the West, demonstrating the truth of their saying: "We are Venetians first, and Christians afterward." They were known for being hospitable and broadminded. "Of all the cities that I have ever known," wrote a French ambassador, "Venice is the one where the greatest honor is paid to the stranger."

On the city's marriage day, one commoner and only one shared the tapestry-covered deck of the Bucentaur with the nobles of Venice and their guests. He was the Grand Manager of the Arsenal, the huge shipyard at Venice, a factory for making ships and cannon which was so large that the walls enclosing it were two miles long. He bore the title of Admiral, although he may never have been farther to sea than he sailed this day on the Bucentaur. And for this occasion, though only a master craftsman, he had on a red satin robe. The small arms and cannon manufactured under his direction were extremely important, for the superiority of the Venetians in sea-battles lay in their marksmanship, and even the smallest galleys mounted fifteen guns.

Right:
The Venetian Doge's glittering procession winds across St. Mark's Square and approaches the waterfront.

The Doge on his golden ship, the Bucentaur, *sails out to celebrate the annual "marriage" of Venice to the Adriatic.*

Mass Production Five Centuries Ago

It was the Venice Arsenal that put shipbuilding on a mass production basis using a system of interchangeable parts. Five hundred years before Henry Ford installed his first assembly line, each plank and mast at Venice was cut to a given size, and a ship was outfitted as it floated from station to station: first masts were set, then rigging attached, then oars and guns put into place, and finally stores put into the hold. And just as today's auto manufacturers have parts centers scattered all over the world, Venice kept spare parts for ships in warehouses from Africa to England.

Men were interchangeable, too. Since the Venetian galleys were built to standardized designs, and men were trained at the Arsenal to sail them, other sailors could replace those lost at sea, and operate efficiently right from the start.

Many thousands of production workers labored within the walls of the Arsenal: ships' carpenters, blacksmiths, caulkers, rope-makers,

22

foundry men. There were also painters and carvers of wood—for elegance was not neglected, even though this early example of mass production could turn out one ship ready for the sea in a hundred days. In fact, to impress a visiting king, the workmen once put a galley together and launched it in two hours.

These workers at the Arsenal were soldiers as well. They made up the first citizen army in Europe. Officered by the same men who were their foremen and inspectors during factory hours, they were so loyal and select a body that the guarding of the Great Council and the Senate of Venice was entrusted to them. The immediate availability of such government troops kept the city remarkably free from rebellion.

The "Lion's Mouth"

Always distrustful of the citizens and of each other, Venice's ruling nobles had two other means of keeping everyone in line. One was

Young men playing at the graceful boxing game of "civettino." A contestant stepped on his foe's feet to keep him in one place.

AQVESTO, VA NO LE NOVIZE IN. IN GONDOLA.

A long-tressed bride in her gondola with members of her wedding party.

a system of spies that penetrated everywhere. The second was the "lion's mouth," a kind of letter box set into the walls of certain buildings. Ornamented with a lion's head, these boxes were innocent enough in themselves but dreaded for their contents: to denounce anyone at all to the authorities, a Venetian had only to drop a letter into one of these lions' mouths. As if to indicate his distaste for an ugly business, the eyes of one such lion were rolled upward, while his slightly open lips were twisted in disapproval. Persons denounced in this way never received an open trial; how many, many times death thus reached out to the innocent, no one will ever know.

The victim might be drawn and quartered, that is, torn into four parts by horses. Or he might be hanged or have his head chopped off in the piazzetta, or square, beside St. Mark's church. Certain red stones there were reserved for the execution of nobles. A highly efficient strangling device had also been installed in the dungeons near by: one quick turn of the crank and the job was done. The most fearsome fate was to be buried alive, head down, legs thrashing the empty air.

It did not pay to become unruly in Venice. The rulers were determined to remain in power and to keep the Serene Republic serene. Still, if one were not the rebellious sort and had no more than a single enemy (a denunciation was supposed to require a pair of witnesses), one managed fairly well. Carnivals eased the tension, and a man might even, on those occasions, mix with his betters, for masks and costumes were great levellers. There was usually much to enjoy: exhibitions of snakes; harpists and guitarists in outlandish rigs; clowns and jugglers. Brilliant religious processions could be seen as they made their way toward the Basilica of St. Mark and there would be pageants to welcome visiting dignitaries. Each guild would appear, its members dressed distinctively and bearing emblems of their trade. Many parades were on the water and all were apt to be accompanied by loud salvoes of artillery from the Arsenal and the fleet. Along the Grand Canal, "the finest street in the world," funerals as well as marriages provided a show as they passed, the former on their way to bury the dead on the cemetery island of San Michele. Poor people had a wry way of saying that on San Michele they would at last become landowners.

Though a worker lived in cramped, small rooms crowded with children and visitors and relatives, he was reasonably content. He was probably a skilled artisan, for Venice was a city of artisans. Her jewelry was the finest in Europe, her mosaics excelled Rome's, and she guarded her secrets. She had learned the art of glass blowing in the East and kept that knowledge to herself as well. It was better for a worker not to be too ambitious, if he had served his apprenticeship in making that delicate Venetian glass. Any worker trying to improve his lot by taking his knowledge of secret processes to some other market was certain to be tracked down and killed. Venice had spies not only at home but all over Europe.

The "Lords of the Night"

After sundown, the city came under the Lords of the Night, six nobles who controlled Venice through the dark hours. Each had a band of assistants to arrest ruffians, thieves and would-be murderers. The Lords of the Night also had additional duties, such as the upkeep

During a carnival, Venetian toughs called "bravoes" brawl as masked revellers ride away.

of the roads, since repairs could be made at night. But why they also had to arrest bigamists and make people pay their rent is not entirely clear.

To a visitor from other Italian cities, all this round-the-clock supervision of the Venetians made them appear somewhat oppressed. Yet many of the controls resulted in public benefits. For example, indiscriminate dumping of filth in the canals was prohibited. What we would call air pollution was controlled; workshops producing unhealthy fumes had to move to uninhabited areas. All food and meat was inspected. Visitors exclaimed over the cleanliness of the streets. Lanterns shed light over dangerous paths. The government checked on water cisterns to make sure they did not let in contamination. Tavern owners were restrained from watering down their wine. Child labor was not forbidden, but where very small children were concerned, it was restricted. In glass blowing, neither boys nor girls could work with emery dust or heated lead.

When a child was born into a Venetian family, the mother would cry out, loud enough to be heard in the street, whether it was a

26

boy or a girl. Elaborate lying-in ceremonies would follow. If the family was well-to-do, the mother's bed coverings would be of woven silver, gold and silk, and her bed jackets frilly with lace, and there would be a splendid array of food for the guests. Finally these receptions became so extravagant that in 1537 the Senate passed a law limiting the guests to relatives. Officials with a search warrant were empowered to enter the house to find out if the guests were really kin.

Most laws favored the nobles, which did not please the great majority of Venetians, since no more than two thousand of the

Street peddlers, called "mountebanks" because they stood on benches, put on a musical act to attract trade.

190,000 residents belonged to the privileged class. However, one law did make for better feeling between patrician families and the rest: a patrician child could not have a noble godfather. Since the child might have as many as one hundred and fifty godfathers, all commoners, this brought commoners into closer contact with some of the nobility.

For christening, the child was carried to the baptismal font under a canopy or lying upon a splendid tray. Its swaddling clothes were decorated with lace, saints' images and medals; among the poorer parents, at least, these were thought to protect the child from being bewitched. Superstition always went further among the poor. It was believed that cutting the infant's nails would cause it to become a thief in later life. Piercing the ear lobes kept the child from having convulsions. Long ears meant a long life.

Brides and Bridegrooms

Rich families saw to it that their sons and daughters married the "right people," for marriage, too, was controlled. Parents arranged the betrothal and settled the size of the bride's dowry. Occasionally a third party acted as go-between and the groom did not see his bride-to-be until the day for signing the marriage contract. The state took an interest in all this, too, checking on the marriage contract and making sure the dowry was not too large. They did this last because the size of the dowries had become such a matter of status that families bankrupted themselves to provide them. Commerce, which was the lifeblood of Venice, suffered, too, because many young men preferred to seek a rich bride rather than to engage in business.

Venetians loved display and, to some, nothing looked more magnificent than bowls full of money placed on the table along with the wedding feast. In one instance the bride's dowry filled six large bowls. The wedding of such a girl might be attended by as many as forty best men. Each of these contributed an expensive gift. The day after the wedding they gave more presents, but not such valuable ones. The customary gift of a best man to the groom was a candy made of pine nuts, sugar and newly-laid eggs. To the bride he would give a sewing basket containing needles of Damascus steel and an engraved ring stand of silver. What a pity if the forty best men all presented the same traditional gifts!

Marriage offered fewer problems to the average Venetian, especially to those who made their living from hard work rather than from

A religious procession in front of St. Mark's church in Venice.

buying and selling. A young man just learning a trade might see a pretty girl in church and find a way to meet her after the service. From then on, his church attendance improved and he also looked for her in the crowds at festivals. The affair became really serious when he serenaded the girl as she sat at her window. For such an occasion he dressed in his holiday best: tight hose, perhaps fastened below the knee with a bow; close-fitting vest and a fancy cap and jacket. His hair would be oiled and carefully combed. He would smell rather strongly of perfume. Most important of all, he would wear a dagger as proof of his manliness.

Later on came the embarrassing moment when he must ask the girl's parents for permission to marry her. If he was accepted, the two families came together at a festive meal and he gave his fiancée a gold ring. Tradition regulated the gifts they received from each other before marriage. She gave him ties and embroidered handkerchiefs. Gifts from him on religious holidays included chestnuts on St. Martin's Day (November 11), almond cakes and relishes for Christmas, a special kind of bun at Easter, and on St. Mark's day, a rosebud.

People were usually married on a Sunday. A typical bridal dress had a white collar of fine cloth above a tight bodice. The full skirt reached to the ground. The bride's dressy apron bore designs in gold thread, and for a necklace she wore a delicate gold chain. These beautiful chains, called *mancini*, were restricted by snobbery to the daughters of Venice's artisans and other workers. The bride tripped

A gibbet with hanging body was a frequent sight.

to the altar in richly embroidered slippers, and when she knelt, might show a glimpse of red petticoats.

The good wife of Venice placed her husband's well-being before her own. She ran to greet him when he returned home, helped him out of his street clothes, saw to it that a meal was ready, and directed the entire household with his comfort in mind.

Mourning the Dead

On the day when a member of the family died, the whole house, and later the streets and church, rang with lamentations. Some of the mourners, following old custom, went unshaven. But Venice, golden

30

bright, was not made for the shadows; there were almost no suicides, and so strong was the feeling against death that no one wearing mourning was allowed to enter the palace of the Doge.

Funerals became sumptuous, too. Bells tolled, or pealed, according to the status, low or high, of the dead. A shop might be closed, or all the shops, again according to the rank of the departed. Walls might be hung with curtains of black velvet fringed with gold. There would be a great procession headed by the guilds with hundreds of banners, the members in red, blue or white, holding tall candles, gilded and painted. There were priests chanting, and members of the household carrying candles around the coffin or bier. Dignitaries followed, and sometimes, for special persons, even the Doge himself, dressed in crimson velvet. Last of all came the people of Venice.

After the service, an orator spoke from a black-draped platform. Darting here and there among the listeners to collect wax candle drippings and put them in a sack around his neck was a man called the *cerone*, from the Italian word for church candle. Fights often broke out between relatives and church authorities over death and burial dues, and even over shares of the wax. As for the bodies, although the poorest might be laid in unmarked graves, those who could afford it were buried in tombs, many resting beneath their own carved likenesses, showing them as they looked in life, not death. Emblems of the dead man's profession might be piled about his coffin: a physician, for instance, would be identified by the books of such ancient healers as Galen or Hippocrates. The Venetian love of pomp and drama tended to transform a sorrow into a splendid pageant. In Venice, the accent was always on life.

An Age of Display

The Renaissance was an age of display, with every man his own showcase. Such an official as Venice's Doge had robes of cloth of gold and on state occasions put on a bonnet studded with jewels and valued at almost 200,000 ducats, or well over half a million dollars. Where eating too much had been one of the seven deadly sins in the Middle Ages, dressing too well now took its place.

Everybody wanted belts and buckles in constantly novel shapes, and a special guild was established to provide them. An ornamental belt clasp might be as large as a child's hand. For the Pope's cape-like outer garment, a button made by a master artist was the size of a small plate. Lace—which Venice is credited with inventing—was in demand even for gloves and shoes as well as for underwear and nightgowns. These last were first used in the sixteenth century, people usually having slept naked before that time. Women wore pattens, an early type of platform shoe, partly to keep their clothing out of the dirt, partly to look taller. The pattens were sometimes so high that their wearers, to avoid falling, had to teeter along leaning on the arm of a servant.

The Dogaressa, wife of the Doge or chief magistrate of Venice, might wear a gown of gold brocade lined with ermine and having a very long train, a gem-studded headdress with a light silken veil attached, enormous diamond and pearl brooches, and a gold belt that tied in front and hung to her feet. Sometimes, for drama, women would dampen down their blazing colors with an overall transparent veil of black.

Isabella d'Este, the brilliant and glamorous Marchesa of Mantua whom Italians called "The First Lady of the World," was so magnificent that the King of France sent word asking her for a wax doll dressed exactly as she was, to show his ladies at home. Just one of her ornaments was a bride's wedding belt that was worked in gold and silver and cost, in our money, well over two thousand dollars.

"We were . . . so magnificently dressed," wrote the famous noblewoman, Lucrezia Borgia, of a formal visit, "that we might have been said to have stripped Florence of all its brocade."

Balloon Sleeves and Scarlet Hose

Not only Italian but many other courts were splendid. England's King

A "glamor girl" of the Renaissance with eye make-up and an elaborate jewelled snood.

Henry VIII wore jewelled rings on both forefingers. He wore a plumed and jewelled hat cocked rakishly on one side, a huge, furred outer coat with great balloon sleeves, a white brocade tunic hung with rubies, and a scabbard heavy with gold for his dagger, to mention only part of his dress. His daughter, the great Queen Elizabeth, wore hoop skirts, huge ruffs stretched on wire, enormous sleeves, blinding jewels. One dress, described in detail by a French ambassador, was black taffeta with gold bands. Down the top of the arms it had sleeve openings (called *finestrelli*, little windows) which were lined with crimson. This dress was open in front all the way to the waist, and the ambassador hardly knew where to look. Elizabeth

Bridal parties reached a peak of elegance in mid-fifteenth century Florence.

34

also had on a long red wig covered with pearls. About her arms were strands of pearls and bracelets of jewels.

One day when Robert Devereux, Earl of Essex—the Queen's favorite in her later years—had just returned from a journey, he burst into her apartments to surprise her. It was, however, Essex who was surprised. He found Elizabeth in the midst of her ladies; she was wearing a simple dressing gown, with no "beauty aids," no wig, and gray hair every which way about her face.

Wigs were much in demand. They were often made of real hair, bought from peasant women who let their hair grow long and then sold it. In Florence and Venice women wore false hair that was

*Fashionable women
teetered along
on platform shoes, or
pattens. Heels had not yet
come into style.*

made out of white and yellow silk. Ordinary people also wore wigs. By way of a joke, a university student living at a boarding house in Paris advised a frequently beaten servant girl how to win her next battle with the landlady. "Next time," he said, "rip off her false curls and grab her hair." At supper time, hearing the noise of women fighting, he ran to separate the combatants. He found them struggling on the floor, ringlets to left of them, caps to right of them—and some floating tufts of the landlady's own hair.

Even the men who rowed gondolas went handsomely dressed. "I hold my sides," wrote Aretino, an Italian literary man who lived in a house overlooking Venice's Grand Canal, "when I listen to the boatmen shouting, jeering, and roaring at those who are rowed by servants who do not wear scarlet hose." Like leotards, such hose ran from a man's feet to his waist and were skin tight. The painter Carpaccio depicts them vividly in his most famous canal scene, where gondoliers in splendid garments glow with many colors from the famous Venetian dye-vats. Most elegant of the boatmen is a handsome young Negro, wearing a tight-fitting red cap with a white plume, a stylish red jacket with a touch of ermine at the shoulders, and patterned hose of silver and green.

Storing all of a noble's garments and other treasures was a problem in itself. Many palaces had an apartment or even a tower called the wardrobe—*guardaroba* in Italian—where clothing, costly plate, weapons, furniture and other valuables were kept. Nobles used to pass hours at a time in the wardrobe.

As for the people, they copied, in much cheaper materials of course, the dress of society's leaders. Instead of pattens on their feet, they wore clogs. Their fans were of straw, with a small piece of looking glass for ornament, whereas those of the rich were of jewel-studded ivory or gold or tortoise-shell, and decorated with feathers, lace and drawings of current events. Some of the clothing commonly seen in Venice, such as the *cafetan*, a long gown with full sleeves, was Eastern in style and name. Whether the Venetians were arsenal workers, dock hands, or peasants at the market, their garments tended to be bright in color and were worn with an air.

Partly because it was felt that people should not dress beyond their station, the commoners were subject to laws which prohibited extravagance, particularly in dress. In Arezzo in 1568 a peasant woman was forbidden to wear any silk except a silk hairnet, a bonnet or some ribbons. The amount of gold cloth that could be used by the richer classes was also regulated. No boy under twelve was allowed to wear a belt made of pearls, and in 1562 a law was passed forbidding a woman who had been married ten years to wear any pearls at all.

But in actual practice these laws were hard to enforce and were often flouted.

Cosmetics—Renaissance Style

Other beautifiers were available. Cosmetics have probably been in use as long as there have been people. In ancient Greece, some women managed to disguise their appearance so well that officials stopped an epidemic of female suicide by decreeing that any woman who had killed herself would be carried naked through the market place. Searching for beauty, Renaissance women endured any agony, even cramming themselves into metal corsets that could be tightened by turning a key. The poet Petrarch said that they suffered as much from vanity as martyrs endure for faith. At night a Venetian belle might improve her complexion by applying a slice of raw veal that had been soaked in milk. Other skin aids included alum, extract of peach stones, lemon juice, bread crumbs, and vinegar distilled with dung. She also used a hair-remover (as did the ancient Greeks and Arabs) containing such ingredients as orpiment, lime, gum arabic and ant eggs.

Women spent long hours on rooftops bleaching their hair on wide-brimmed, crownless hats.

The dressing table of a noble lady would be covered with comb cases, hair brushes with gilt backs, golden tweezers, dozens of rouge pots to color cheeks and bosom. A poet of the people wrote that ladies spent their whole day in front of the mirror, and complained that women of his class were beginning to imitate them. Women dyed their hair, preferring to be blonde, which in Venice often meant auburn. Fashionable men also appeared with dyed hair, and even with two different colors on successive days. Drying their hair, ladies would sit, mirror in hand, on the roof, wearing a loose dressing gown and a huge, crownless straw hat, with their hair spread out on the brim. They polished their nails, painted and plastered their faces, eyelids and even teeth. Among the cosmetics of the Marchesa of Mantua was a special recipe for washing the teeth that had been used by the Queens of Naples. Queen Elizabeth's teeth blackened as she aged, and she might have done well to send for this "toothpaste." Indeed, the lack of proper dentistry made people look old before their time, their faces shrunken, their noses and chins coming too close together.

Perfumes were a necessity. Foul smells, although doubtless not so harmful as our polluted air, tainted the Renaissance air. Pigsties, offal, urine, slaughterhouses, poulterers' and fishmongers' establishments, added their aromas. One day when the great Protestant

37

reformer, Martin Luther, had not been able to attend church, he inquired of his wife Katherine as to whether the church had been full. "So full it stank," was Katherine's answer. A traveler might object to many smells, including those of English dining halls, where the floors were covered with none-too-clean rushes or straw. Among other smells, common enough in that age of no refrigerators, was that of salt fish. Venice was particularly smelly—especially when the canals were awash with garbage—and the Venetians were among the best customers for incense imported from the Orient. In the fifteenth century a still more expensive remedy was tried: someone got the idea of mixing spices with earth and packing this down on various paths and open spaces. During plague times the smell of sick and dead bodies and of medicines was such that people warded it off with flowers, fragrant herbs and other scents. When people in Rome were dying at the rate of at least one hundred a day a courtier wrote: "All I can do is to wash in vinegar, perfume my hands, and commend my soul to God—at home, not in church."

An Italian lady might make her own perfumes, putting them up

Gorgeously attired lords and ladies are entertained by acrobats, wrestlers and lute players.

A ballroom scene at the court of Henry III of France at the start of an era of high fashion.

in silver boxes for her friends. Everything, even to a roll of money, would be scented by those who could afford it. People carried prayer-beads of sweet-smelling amber or smelling bottles, and tucked about their persons a "pouncet-box," which had a perforated lid and was filled with perfumed unguents. For ceremonial processions, even the mules were rubbed with perfume. In the practice of witchcraft, precious scents were used to summon up demons and foul-smelling asafetida was used to repel them. Cinnamon and peppermint scents were added to bath water. Before and after a banquet, rose water from a silver ewer was poured on the hands of the guests. Although appealing first to the eye, Renaissance people wished to delight the other senses as well.

The Rise of Women

Women had much to do with the splendid display and the increasing refinement of manners typical of this period. But they were not sufficiently valued. As the Renaissance phrased it, woman was "a half-man, a man marred in the making." Men and women alike were taught at an early age that maleness was superior to femaleness, and that man was the "head" and ruler of woman. Besides, woman was more sinful than man; seduced by the Devil, Eve had brought about the Fall of Man; she had lured Adam into tasting the forbidden apple, and for this the human race was expelled from Paradise. Since women were sinful they deserved to suffer—and we can say without fear of contradiction that men contributed to their punishment.

Man ruled, woman was his property, and he was free to humiliate, strike and even murder her. We read with horror of King Henry VIII having two of his six wives put to death, but any wife or daughter might be killed by a husband or father in those days. Women were constantly spied on and denounced. A not unusual case was that of Parisina Malatesta, beautiful and accomplished, whose husband, an Italian marquis, eavesdropped on her by drilling a hole in the ceiling of her room. Learning in this way of Parisina's love for his son by an earlier wife, the marquis had them both decapitated. The following jingle summed up the usual view:

A woman, a dog, and a walnut tree,
The more you beat 'em, the better they be.

As for a husband remaining faithful to his wife, this was seldom heard of. Prostitution, substitute wives, illegitimacy, were the order of the day. Slavery also existed: slaves were valuable property, and they were usually better treated than servants. Many bore children to the head of the house. Most wives put up with all this.

The birth of a girl was no cause for rejoicing. The parents knew that they would soon have to provide her with a dowry, since men had to be bribed to marry. As Machiavelli, the famous author of *The Prince*, pointed out: "Those who live with and maintain women have both the good of them and the bother . . . always a fly in the honey." Convents required a smaller entrance fee than marriage, so fathers often chose this means of disposing of a daughter. Such convents were in a way fashionable homes for gentlewomen; like some monasteries in England, they could be well run and comfortable.

Girls were married off at an early age, for men preferred brides as young as twelve. But some aristocratic families kept their daughters

Love in a secluded garden, around 1490.

40

at home till they were seventeen. Marriage as a rule was not based on love, but was simply a business transaction arranged by the families. After an extravagant wedding—a matter of family pride—many girls found themselves matched to total strangers.

Learned Ladies

Women could rise only through education and struggle. But for a woman to get an education was very difficult. Most men of the day, including churchmen, scholars and educators, stood together against women, and constantly spoke of them with contempt. The chancellor of the University of Paris said: "All instruction for women should be looked at askance." An Italian philosopher remarked: "I allow woman to learn; to teach, never." A great Dutch scholar said of the education of girls: "Topsy-turvidom." And a French chronicler added, "From a braying mule and a girl who speaks Latin, good Lord deliver us."

In spite of all this, we can truthfully speak of the rise of women during the Renaissance. Spain was known as the country of learned women. The girls there were said to absorb Latin with their mother's milk. This was partly the result of the Saracen influence after the Muslims—followers of the Prophet Muhammad—invaded Spain in 711. Saracen women had fared considerably better than the rest. Although the desert Arabs before the Prophet Muhammad considered their newborn daughters worthless and used to bury them alive, Muhammad granted spiritual equality to men and women. So advanced were Saracen ladies that when the French

Right:
Young ladies weaving and embroidering. Since high foreheads were considered beautiful, the hairlines of girls were plucked or shaved.

A woman litigant before a judge.

42

wished to praise Marguerite, a little princess of thirteen, highly accomplished and well educated, they said of her that she was "rather Persian than French." A tutor in Spain named Vivès educated the four daughters of Queen Isabella. Afterward, traveling to England, he aroused enthusiasm for educating girls. As a result, the girls of England's court were well trained. At fourteen, the future Queen Elizabeth translated "The Mirror of the Sinful Soul," a work by Marguerite of France.

Educated women formed academies where they read orations and essays to audiences of both sexes, or engaged in debates. There were women painters, teachers and governesses. The pupils of one teacher, Olympia Morata, all noble young girls under fifteen, read philosophy, studied mathematics, and learned the map of the world. They also learned to act, and presented a comedy before the Pope.

High-born girls were brought up to supervise their future house-holds and servants. They knew and practiced some medicine, which did not always please the doctors. Along with collecting herbs and learning to cook, they made healing mixtures as well as cosmetics. They embroidered, were given religious books, had dolls, played games, and went to church—one of their few chances to see and be seen. They played the lute, harp and zithern, and sang and danced. The literature of southern France, called Provençal, and of Spain, and Italian novels were their delight; Authors old and new, Virgil and Horace, Dante, Petrarch and Boccaccio were popular, and an Italian poem, *Arcadia*, ran into sixty editions. They also read much trash; stories about dead knights coming to life, a warrior killing a hundred foes, a widow dying of grief, enchanted them.

The educator Vivès did not approve of all this. For girls he advocated cold water, a vegetarian diet, and hard study, rather than sentimentalities. No dancing or romancing: he stood for the Scriptures, history, ethics, and Greek philosophy. Joke books and the sensual, immoral side of learning, were not for girls, he said; he would rather see a girl "deaf or blind than over-stimulated to pleasure." Meanwhile as their elders criticized them for loading their fingers with rings—above the joint as well as below—piercing their ears, overdoing their dress, makeup and perfumes, the girls laughed and flirted away their youth. Love letters, secret meetings, and tokens of affection were the rule. They were well-mannered, addressing their mothers as "Madam, my mother," and saying "By your favor, Madam," and learning to approach their betrothed with "Sir, my good friend," and to sign a letter to a husband with, "Your wife and subject."

Life was probably both better and worse for women then. Some

Dancing the lively galliard.

city women were successful in business. Many learned a trade, such as tailoring, brewing and manufacturing silk. The latter has long been associated with women. Silk manufacturing was for many centuries a carefully-guarded secret of the Chinese; one legend—among several—says a Chinese princess finally carried it to India by concealing silk worms or their eggs, and mulberry leaves or seeds, in her hair. In time it made a livelihood for the women silk workers of London. Fourteenth century records show that four percent of London's taxpayers were women.

Meanwhile, women were spending more time in the company of men, traveling with them as the roads became better and safer, eating at table with them, influencing their art and other work. Their presence hastened an improvement in social behavior. Late in the thirteenth century diners were advised to wipe their mouth

A portable organ being played at a garden party.

neatly with the table cloth after drinking, and not to clean their ears with their fingers during the meal. Each diner was provided with his own personal sheathed knife, and a slice of bread served as a plate. During the fourteenth century, however, table napkins came in. Diners were urged not to scratch at table, and told that if they had to spit, to do it politely. Other admonitions were: if you have taken a bite out of a fruit, don't offer the fruit to your neighbor; don't wear your toothpick in your collar; and don't put your foot on the table.

Forks were still rare, but it was a woman who had introduced them to Venice, as far back as the eleventh century. She was a Greek princess from Constantinople, who never touched food with her fingers, but lifted it to her mouth on a golden, two-pronged fork. Condemned for such luxurious ways, she died of a terrible disease, which people felt she deserved.

First Ladies

Some women of the Renaissance were good fighters, too, putting on armor and leading troops against male aggressors. Most admirable, however, were the statesmanlike women who ruled officially or unofficially as regents or co-sovereigns. There was Louise of Savoy, mother of Francis I of France, who served as regent in his place; Isabella of Spain, to whom the discovery of America was largely due; Elizabeth of England, for whom an age was named; Isabella d'Este, who wrote her husband: "I beg of you, keep a tranquil mind . . . for I intend to govern the state . . . and all that is possible will be done for the good of our subjects."

Although history, written by men, has largely overlooked the accomplishments of women, the leading ladies of the Renaissance asked for and received much masculine adulation. They enjoyed being called "a new Helen of Troy" or "First Lady of the World." Less agreeable were the constant instructions from men on how they should act, dress, and be. One author solemnly directed them to "put on the slippers of humility, the shift of decorum, the corset of chastity, the garters of steadfastness and the pins of patience. . . ."

To sum up, the women of that day, although on the march, were still a long way from achieving equality with men. For this women would have to wait another four hundred years.

Chess was called "an exercise worthy of fine wits and noble birth." Women often played against men.

47

5 How They Lived and Played

The poor of Italian cities liked their children to have dirty hands and feet, believing that this protected them from serious illness. When washing could not be avoided the mother hurried to her favorite shrine and breathed a prayer to protect the child until he regained a healthy amount of dirt. This did not take long. The children played in the streets, which were nearly as filthy as they had been in medieval times. Travelers commented often on the cleanliness of Italian towns, yet this cleanliness was only relative. By modern standards, they were dirty. Slops and garbage of all kinds were thrown into the streets and alleys, except in Venice where they were emptied into the canals. City authorities had begun banning livestock from roaming at will, but this had its drawbacks: it meant that pigs could no longer act as scavengers.

Games and other entertainments, processions and pranks were part of street life, but the main use of European downtown streets and squares was for business. Traders in the same commodity tended to gather in one area, and streets were named for the occupations found in them. Thus, *Getreidegasse* in Salzburg, Austria, means Grain Street and recalls the time when grain merchants monopolized it. Similar names—Haymarket in London, for example—refer to long-vanished uses. Craftsmen liked to have their workshops on the ground floor and facing the street. By fastening hinges to the bottom edge of a window shutter they could let the shutter down in the daytime and use it as a counter to display their goods. Some craftsmen took up too much of the street, so regulations were made to limit their encroachments. On the other hand, members of the powerful wool guild were permitted to hang dripping wool above the street. Hanks of billowing yarn and lengths of cloth drying at nearly every window gave sections of Florence a carnival air, but even the wariest passerby sometimes received an unwanted shower. In such districts iron supports were fastened to each side of a window, then wooden cross bars laid over the bars to hold the cloth. Even private houses were fitted out in this way.

As soon as the sun went down almost all activity in a town came to a stop. Shopkeepers took in their wares, put up shutters and bolted them fast. Town gates closed, children vanished, the traditional cries of hawkers ceased, smiths and carpenters put down their hammers. Where there had been a constant din, there was now a strange calm. Guild rules prohibited night work and set heavy fines

48

for violators. In the silk guild no one was allowed to touch the cocoons from night till morning. Entertainments were daytime affairs except for the rich and on a few special occasions. Residents went inside their houses, closed their doors tight, ate their evening meal, played on a lute, perhaps, and sang. Since candles were expensive, most citizens went to bed fairly soon after the workday had ended. Only a few braved the dark streets. Nobility and officials passed to and from social affairs or business of state accompanied by body-guards with torches, and with weapons at the ready.

Italian homes ranged from lean-tos built against a ruined wall, through country villas among cypress trees and flower gardens, to palaces that made the French invaders of the sixteenth century gaze in awe. The French tried to hide their amazement at so much luxury, but the king himself had rarely seen anything to equal the splendid mansions of Florentine businessmen. Palace rooms were huge, with ornaments on all surfaces, including the window shutters, which were often covered with richly embroidered cloth. The floors would be paved with decorative tiles or marble in geometric designs; walls

Above left:
A wedding of commoners.
A canopy keeps off the hot
Italian sun.

Above right:
A sixteenth-century
kitchen. Poultry hangs out
of a cat's reach. Beside the
oven are paddles for
removing bread. Dough is
being rolled for macaroni
and spaghetti at center table.

Taking an inventory of household goods.

would be hung with costly tapestries, or bear paintings by the artists most in vogue. Ceilings might be vaulted and covered with frescoes, or flat, with deeply recessed panels that glowed with color. The furniture was handsomely designed, intricately carved, and built to last through several lifetimes. Silver dishes and vases, just then coming into fashion, would be on display. So, too, would Venetian glass and ceramics. Color and gilt would strike the eye from every angle.

Where the Workmen Lived

But what about the man who carved the furniture or the one who fired the kiln where the ceramics were glazed? Where did such a man live?

Because so many wanted to stay within the protecting walls of a town, most people lived in small, overcrowded rooms. Steep and narrow stairs led from one floor to the next and water for washing and cooking had to be carried up from a well in the courtyard or a fountain in a nearby square. Living quarters like these rarely had more than a few small windows per family. In winter, solid wooden shutters covered them to keep out the cold, leaving the rooms in darkness or fitfully lit from the fireplace or smelly open-wick lamps that sputtered in fat because tallow for candles was expensive. In summer, the shutters were left open and flying insects were kept out by means of oiled linen stretched on wooden frames. All cooking was done in the fireplace, which usually had a hood to carry off the smoke and steam. In better homes this hood might be decorated with artistic designs. Pots were fashioned with legs so that they could straddle the small fire—small because wood was not cheap. A fifteenth-century list of objects in a Siena doctor's kitchen adds such items as a pair of gridirons; a stamp for marking things belonging to the house; a pair of mustard grinders; three pictures; two small cups of pewter and two pewter molds; a salt box, a small table with wooden legs, and a safe for salted meat.

Families ate in the kitchen and many of them used it for a bedroom as well. Since their dining tables ordinarily consisted of boards laid across trestles, these could easily be removed to make more room. People sat on benches rather than chairs when at table, a chair being reserved as a seat of honor—hence our term chairman. Two of the benches could be placed together to form a narrow bedstead, but the more usual bed for sleeping in a kitchen was a crude mattress laid on the floor.

In cities with more space, as in Venice, a worker's home was quite cheerful. The rooms would still be small but a two-story house frequently had a balcony across the front with a vine growing up to the eaves. Possibly there would be a tiny garden with some fruit trees. The more skilled artisans enjoyed polished floors of imitation marble and they had brass platters and copper kettles to decorate the kitchen, and walnut bedsteads and chests in the other rooms.

Working people owned little furniture beyond what was in the kitchen; beds and chests made up most of it. Houses were built without closets, so that chests were essential for storage. They could also be sat upon, and even used for a bed. A wife treasured her *cassone*, the chest which she had brought to her new home as a bride, and which, being part of her dowry, was as elegantly decorated as the family could afford.

The bride of a well-to-do merchant would bring with her a beautifully painted wedding chest and would come into a home with fairly large rooms. Each room would open into the next in a sort of maze, since few houses had corridors. A guest might have to pass through several other bedrooms to reach his own, but no one was disturbed by this, privacy being a relatively modern idea. Late-sleepers frequently awoke in the midst of family activities, for rooms, even among those people who were well off, often served more than one purpose. Thus a pleasant or convenient bedroom might turn into the sitting room before the bed's occupants were awake.

Beds, Chairs and Stoves

Beds were symbols of one's status. An elaborate bedroom might be hung with velvet and cloth of gold, while the bed itself had covers worked in silver, and bolsters of silk. A bedstead might be inlaid with precious stones: lapis lazuli, cornelian, agate, crystal. To a degree, the higher the bed, the richer the owner; exceptions were beds in Holland and the Swiss Alps which consisted of berthlike cubicles built against the wall and reached by mounting a step or a short ladder.

The "king-size" bed is not a modern innovation, for the beds of the rich began to expand in the fifteenth century until some of them were as much as eight feet long and seven feet wide. With a canopy over them, and curtains let down on all four sides, such beds were a room within a room, protecting the occupants from cold drafts. In time, these beds became free-standing four-posters, which were easier to construct and move about.

Not even a king had mattress springs to ease his nights. Mattresses were large cloth bags stuffed with straw, or goose down, or dried pea hulls, or even leaves. Small wonder that when they traveled, Europe's rich brought their own beds with them. Their luggage also included a ceremonial chair in which the important traveler sat at table or received his guests. An emblem of authority, the chair was more impressive than comfortable, having a high, straight back and a small canopy, but no upholstery. During the Renaissance, the chair lost its exclusiveness; no longer reserved for a duke, a bishop, the head of a household or a business, it came into general use. Since a hard oak seat did not appeal to burghers, they added cushions covered with leather, velvet or silk. The furniture makers, now freed from making the throne type of chair, sometimes went

to extremes: one of them produced a chair that could be changed into a bed, couch or table; another delighted practical jokers with a chair that trapped anyone who sat down on it.

The same ingenuity helped to solve the heating problem. The Germans, ever on the lookout for comfort, introduced the stove to a world that had been kept busy warming its hands at fireplaces while its rear was freezing. Other countries were quick to see the advantage of a stove over a fireplace which allowed most of the heat to escape up the chimney. Stoves began to appear in middle-class homes throughout Europe, and no other Renaissance invention contributed so much to human well-being. One unusual application of the principle that heat rises was noted by a traveler in Poland. He tells of a house where several holes had been cut through the ceiling above a stove. Instead of gathering around this stove the

The birth of a baby. The newborn infant will be wrapped tight in swaddling clothes to keep its limbs straight.

Youngsters at play.

family would go upstairs and sit over the holes on special chairs with open seats.

Stoves also reduced, without eliminating, the danger of fire, because fireplaces were the chief cause of houses burning to the ground. What with all the hangings on walls and beds, the windows of oiled cloth, the rushes or straw matting on the floors, there was plenty to burn. Cities established fire wardens in cathedral towers or other high places to watch for the dreaded flames and sound the alarm; some of these watchers, in a town built of pine wood, would sing out at intervals through the night. Strasbourg in Alsace-Lorraine seems to have had one of the best fire brigades; there three men in the cathedral tower took turns as lookouts. Each district was under its captain, and each man knew his exact duties. As soon as an alarm was sounded some of the firemen ran to the blaze with pails of water, axes, iron hooks and long pikes. Others brought sacks stuffed with straw to break the fall of persons jumping from the house. As a safety measure, one official recommended that each householder keep a strong rope down which he could slide in time of peril.

Looters swarmed to fires, and not infrequently started them. A man's personal enemies might also set his house on fire. Occasionally a city government burned out a district known to oppose the régime. If by ill-luck the houses of their own supporters burned, too, the owners would be reimbursed.

Keeping Clean

Nothing has been said about bathing in the Renaissance, because little was done about it. People did bathe, some of them every few weeks. Between times they took "sponge baths." A small room on the courtyard might serve for a real bath, or, in a palace, a bathing alcove might have a tub and perhaps a canopy and curtains. Two or more persons might sit in a large wooden tub, perhaps sharing a tray of food laid across it. There might also be musicians playing near by. The tub was filled with hot water by hand. Most of the time people washed only their hands, face and teeth, and bedrooms were sometimes provided with a basin and pitcher for this purpose. In this or other rooms there might be a laver, that is, a fixed stone basin with a container of water hooked up above it; a faucet worked by a small handle released the water. Such sinks or basins might empty through a drain pipe to the street. In monasteries, some of which had good water systems, monks were expected to wash so well that they would not get dirt on the towel. At table, diners washed their hands before and after meals, ewers and basins being used for the purpose; sometimes the water was strewn with rose petals. There was also, of course, some wiping on beard or robe. Although soap was first manufactured in England in the fourteenth century, we do not hear much of it in the early Renaissance. Generally speaking, baths continued to be thought of as an event rather than routine procedure; and some even looked askance at such people as the Danes who bathed every Saturday. Hot water was always available at public baths, but these places, called stews, were avoided by many, for they were often frequented by undesirable persons.

As a rule, there were no indoor toilets in the average house. When there was a narrow space between two buildings, planks might be laid from wall to wall, making a precarious latrine into which the unwary sometimes fell. Great houses, castles or monasteries built "privy closets" into their walls, and from the fourteenth century on, chamber pots were tucked about the house, and even hidden in dining room cupboards. In Edinburgh, such receptacles were emptied out the window, early in the morning, with the warning cry: "Gardy-loo!" (from the French *gare l'eau*, meaning *look out for the water*). The City Guard would later clean out the streets, except on the Sabbath. There were also "nightmen" in London who, from cesspits and elsewhere, carried off soil to farmers or to a communal dump. Sir John Harington, a godson of Queen Elizabeth, invented the first so-called water closet, a room containing a toilet with a flush device. But not for two centuries was anything like this in common use. At Hampton Court, a typical Renaissance luxury was the lidded, portable "close stool," covered with crimson velvet and trimmed with lace.

Generally speaking, the people of that day, who after all had the same basic needs as we have, saw to them ingeniously enough. They lacked our technological devices, and used more labor, but achieved the same results. Their houses may not have been "machines for living," but served them adequately, and they did not miss what they had never had or never even imagined.

Dwarfs and Jesters

When it came to pleasures and relaxation, the people of the Renaissance found much to enjoy. For example, they loved dwarfs. Although cherished, dwarfs do not seem to have been regarded as complete human beings. People rounded up the tiny men and women and even bred them as pets. An Italian lady wrote a friend to promise her "the first girl born to my dwarfs." Dwarfs often doubled as jesters and buffoons and similar entertainers. If a person was born a pleasing freak, he was assured a comfortable berth for life. A court dwarf named Morgantino was a skilled dancer; on a journey he danced "morescoes" or Moorish dances to amuse the peasants along the way, or joined them in their own country dances. Delighted, they crowned him with leaves and flowers. In the Castle at Mantua there was a whole suite of apartments with low rooms, a chapel and corridors built especially for dwarfs. One of the dwarfs, Mattello, was a gifted mimic and clown; he would dress up in friar's clothes and preach, or would imitate a drunk. When the Lady Isabella's brother was in deep grief because he had lost his wife, Isabella loaned him Mattello. Her brother commented that this loan had done him more good than if someone had given him a castle. Not long afterward, Mattello sickened and died, but even on his deathbed he

joked and clowned. A court poet, mixing Christian and pagan ideas immortalized Mattello: he wrote that if the dwarf had gone to Heaven, he was making the saints and angels laugh; and if he had gone to Hell, the watchdog Cerberus would forget to bark.

Prized hunting dogs being doctored. Wide collars protected their throats from the teeth of their prey.

Pampered Pets

People also kept many pets. Squirrels, rabbits, monkeys, ermine, and tame, free birds were favorites. The birds included parrots and "sports" such as a white lark. A man might go out bird-snaring with cages on his back, while another might buy a caged bird on purpose to set it free. Caged crickets were popular as pets, and so also caged nightingales. It was customary to bring pets into church, and on cold days such little animals may well have served as muffs. Lap dogs, rabbits and even hawks were sometimes among those present. Well-to-do families would own hundreds of dogs, including farm dogs and hunting dogs. A dying noble might send for his greyhounds to see them one last time. A man might have a big, shaggy watchdog who also doubled as a pointer and retriever. Bloodhounds, then as now, were used to track down escaped prisoners.

Cats were a necessity rather than a pet. Nuns who were ordered to keep no animals might keep cats, and cats were also needed on shipboard to thin out the rats. An account notes that three hundred cat skins besides the skins of other small animals were found on a Spanish ship seized off the coast of England. It is probable that cat skins were used to cure various ailments; one can still see these skins in French pharmacies today.

Most rulers with any style had zoos. One Pope was pleased to receive from a Portuguese embassy a white elephant that was brought from India and genuflected three times on meeting His Holiness. The zoos were private and might contain wolves, ferrets, porcupines, bears, tigers and lions. There were some wild animals in cages at the Tower of London, but in Florence they were left loose in a court with high walls. Ferrara had stags, goats, gazelles and giraffes. There

Carnival revelers about to attack each other with eggshells filled with perfumed water. On the right are two masked jugglers.

were also collections of herons, hawks, doves and jays. Swans for moats, lake trout for the table, and long-lived carp for palace pools were among the other animal guests, and so were ostriches and peacocks. The strangest group of pets, however, was a human menagerie: Cardinal Ippolito de' Medici had a collection of "barbarians" of twenty different nationalities, all best of breed.

Games and Dances

Renaissance children paddled in brooks and dammed up the water and floated improvised toy boats. They made mud pies and collected shells. Sometimes they caught butterflies. They had dolls and marbles and tops, blew soap bubbles from a pipe, and rode a stick, calling it a horse. Babies made adults laugh with their new words; in Italy their vocabulary included *Babbo* and *Mamma*, *bombo* for wine, and *dindi* for little coins.

Some games were probably much like games today. In one of them, a kind of tag, you pinched somebody's arm and shouted. Another was "hoodman blind," now blind-man's buff—played with a hood covering the face. There were archery, wrestling, running, jumping, putting the stone. There were all kinds of ball games: a rough football played in the streets, and a sort of croquet where wooden balls were struck with hooked sticks, and *palla* or an early form of

59

Villagers dancing and playing a game that is a combination of bowling and croquet.

cricket, in which a ball was hit with a flat board. Tennis was popular; and the walled courts built in many towns, which also provided for spectators, were often converted into theaters.

A popular jousting game involved the quintain, which was a post, or figure of a Saracen warrior, with revolving arms. A man would run up to it and strike it with a lance; unless his blow was aimed exactly right, an arm of the quintain would strike him back. Baiting bulls and bears—which meant harassing them to death with dogs—is

fortunately no longer common; nor is cock-throwing, or tying a rooster to a post and throwing sticks at it.

People of all classes enjoyed themselves in the pools at water resorts, men and women together, the women struggling to catch floral crowns and coins tossed down by admirers in the gallery above. In places where it snowed and rivers froze, artists might make snow lions, and everyone rode horseback, or skated, or played games on the ice. They even bound the thigh bones of animals to their feet, and, like skiers, propelled themselves forward with iron-tipped poles. Others preferred kissing games, guessing games, and formal debates about love. Both men and women played chess; Queen Elizabeth's chesspieces were of gold, while Italian nobles had chessboards of gold, silver or precious stones, and chess pieces of crystal. People also played with dice, some loaded; and they played checkers, and "tables," a kind of backgammon. Among fashionable card games was one called "raising dead men" and another known as scartino, at which Italians were wont to gamble, whether at home or abroad.

Noble ladies, educated primarily for leisure, had much to amuse them. They sat in the garden under the lemon trees and did embroidery; they listened to master storytellers reciting fairy tales; or they sometimes joined in water-parties, bobbing downstream in lovely boats while an orchestra of court musicians floated after them. They read French poetry, and translations of Spanish and French romances. They knew all about the heroes of Charlemagne, and about Roland, too brave to call for help at first, sounding his

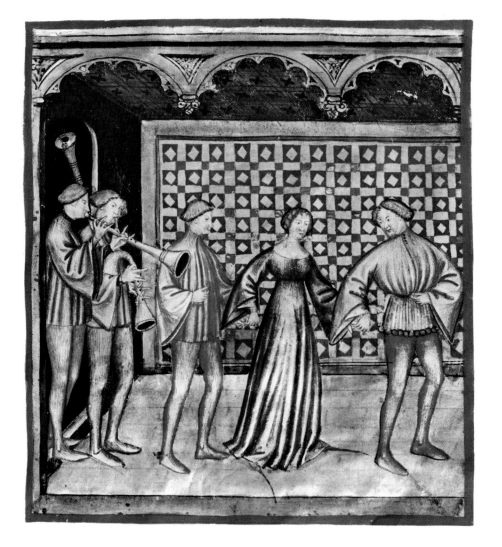

Singers and dancers on a stage.

62

Hunting the unicorn. The prey is imaginary, but the details are true. As in a real hunt, kennelmen and beaters round up the game.

horn as he died. The ladies also had great writers at their beck and call, and enjoyed the society of leading scholars, who, bearing them in mind, tended to write in Italian and in other native languages rather than Latin. From infancy, well-bred girls were taught music and dancing, and could sing sonnets while they played the clavichord, lute or viol.

Dancing was considered an important accomplishment, and besides Jewish comedians and musicians, Jewish dancing masters were much in demand. The French were mad about dances, and had hundreds of them, accompanied by singing, posturing and pantomime. Their basic dance, the galliard, accompanied by oboe and tambourine,

63

was stately, but many of their dances featured leaping and contortions as well. A young girl was taught how to hold her arm so as to display it best, how to lift her robe just a little in order to show off her foot, and how to stretch her mantle away from her to exhibit the cloth. She learned to be light on her feet, dignified and gracious, "with eyes neither wandering nor fixed on a particular gentleman."

In Renaissance Europe, from the sweaty, boisterous peasant dancers in a village square to the perfumed noble swirling sedately under a ceiling painted by a master, men and women danced, both together and apart, by candlelight or torchlight, indoors and out.

Carnivals and Pageants

A good deal of living went on in the streets, especially since houses were apt to be cramped.

There was much to be seen outside: hacked-off human segments exhibited at a city gate; a royal bride or a prince of the church welcomed with a parade; ambassadors or prisoners of war passing by. There were workshops open to the street, and there were fights, and lovers slipping away and thinking themselves unobserved. One could watch the news as it happened. People strolled about, parading up and down at certain hours, or conducting their business, or going out into the countryside.

Carnival—a word probably meaning "take away meat"—was the period of public revelry just before the abstinence of Lent. At carnival time a city went wild. Houses were left empty, open to thieves. Pickpockets also abounded. Since revellers wore costumes and masks, only a few would be caught, especially as the authorities were revelling too. Strangers linked hands and danced around bonfires in the squares. Others, even in Italy, chased bulls through the narrow streets, or they hit each other with eggshells filled with perfumed water—and it wasn't always perfumed. Gangs of boys would pelt each other with stones, or as the carnival season approached, they would get up on a bridge with no railings, start a fist fight and try to knock each other off.

The great carnival parade featured a series of cars or floats passing beneath triumphal arches and carrying historical or symbolic figures to the tune of special carnival songs. These floats were also seen in the public "Triumphs" held at Florence. Not all such spectacles were gay. A popular "Triumph of Death" showed a black float drawn by oxen and piled with skeletons. To solemn music, the skeletons would rise and sing a song of death.

An Italian noblewoman swings a bat in an early form of tennis.

Whether religious or secular, these pageants were something like movable outdoor dramas for all to watch, from every vantage point: windows, rooftops, ledges, trees. The fronts of houses were hung with tapestries or precious oriental rugs, and in some towns the streets were strewn with flowers. At night, during Easter time, colored lights were set in windows, hundreds of lights from story to story, the effect being created by putting candles in little lanterns of dyed paper.

Something in the Renaissance heart craved splendor and display. The rich and powerful wished to dazzle one another and the crowd; they longed for the envy of their equals and the gaping wonder of the masses, and chose to impress by the creation of beautiful things.

A snowball fight between noble lords and ladies.

Overleaf:
A prince with his hunting party on a stag hunt. It was beneath him to kill a doe.

Great artists were employed to create even temporary displays. At the court of Milan, the duties of Leonardo da Vinci, the great artist and all-around Renaissance man, included everything from decorating the Duchess's bathroom to designing public spectacles. For a tourney, he planned the costumes, the belts to be worn, and even the sword hilts. He applied himself to making animal figures filled with air, that floated while the air held out. One of his famous "flying machines" was designed to make an angel on a carnival float flap its wings. No wonder he complained that in order to earn a living for himself and his six apprentices he had to occupy himself with trifles.

Other features of pageants and processions would include the beautifully-designed banners of various guilds; groups of dancers; bands of musicians; prancing horses with cropped ears; and, in parts of England, wickerwork giants. The populace on such occasions could also watch various side-events and feats. There were not only horse races but races featuring such contestants as women, children, or naked old men. Groups of young athletes formed a human pyramid. Or two men, each waiting on a different tower, slid down a separate rope and met at the same instant before the cathedral doors. There might even be fountains running wine; or the royal cooks might provide candy figures in colored and gilded sugar. Probably only a chosen few would get to enjoy other performances, such as that of the buffoon who could swallow a whole pigeon at one mouthful or forty eggs in succession.

A hunt might be organized as part of the festivities. The ladies would sit on a hillside, while beaters, forming a circle, closed in on the game. Hounds, pointer dogs, and crossbows were beginning to replace the hawks; for one thing, hawks could not be used while they were moulting. Sometimes, with as many as two thousand sportsmen and their servants taking part, a canvas enclosure would be spread over a wide area and the beaters would drive in deer, wild boar, wolves, goats, stags, to be shot, or killed with spears. Day after day, the slaughter would go on, ox-carts carrying off the kill.

There were also tourneys, although the jousts were gradually giving way to displays of skill and horsemanship, still to be seen today in Vienna's Spanish Riding School.

Plays and the Golden Age of Song

Besides pages who could recite poetry, and choir singers, and jesters, most courts also employed troupes of actors to put on plays. The plays would be staged in a palace hall or courtyard; a temporary platform might also be set up in a church or on a cart drawn by oxen and supplied with screens of boughs. Some plays were Latin comedies (tragedies were not popular), rather immoral, and some, in Italian, referred to current events. Religious subjects, acted by a guild or "mystery," were still to be seen, as were medieval "miracle plays" featuring wonder-working saints, but these were being replaced by non-religious dramas. In the masques or "mummeries," dramatic entertainments revived from classical times, the actors wore masks and represented mythical and allegorical characters. The people also loved farces, and a type of theater developed that was called the *commedia dell'arte*, which means comedies improvised by members of the actors' "art" or trade; here the story was merely outlined, and the actors made things up as they went along. In Venice people were so much in love with the theater that they would swim canals, climb walls and break down doors to see a famous comedian on the stage.

What the noble audiences liked best about a play were the music and dance interludes: there were fine Morris—meaning Moorish—dances between the acts, the "Moors" holding up lighted torches. Or there would be a harvest ballet, simulating peasants at their various tasks in the fields, and all danced to bagpipes. The music of the Renaissance, once lost, has in recent years been uncovered in monasteries and ancient castles, and reconstructed from old, stained manuscripts without staff lines or indications of pitch. We now know how music sounded at the court of Ferdinand and Isabella; how widespread was the influence there of Arab poetry and song and instruments, and how many European styles grew out of them. Today even the original instruments are being re-introduced: the rebec, a fiddle; the psaltery, a kind of zither; the pandora, an early guitar; the vielle, a sort of violin (later, a "hurdy-gurdy" or wheel viol); and the krummhorn and kortholt, belonging to the oboe family.

In Elizabeth's England everybody was singing madrigals, three-part or four-part songs, and many could read the music at sight. The German *Lied* grew out of French song in the early sixteenth century. In general, the Renaissance was the "Golden Age of Song." But a great change-over was beginning, from religious to popular music, and from voices to instruments.

The word opera means work, the Latin singular being *opus*. Opera is a collection of "works" or arts, such as singing, acting, dancing and instrumental music, all together. Italy gets the credit for inventing opera in the modern sense, the first of these musical

Hunting porcupines. The dog at left is stuck with quills.

dramas being given at Florence in 1597 and 1599. The average Florentine loved music. Blind beggars, young apprentices, everybody sang. The ordinary artisan might hear lute and lyre, harp and horn, organ, harpsichord and violin, Jew's harp and kettledrum, cello, bagpipes and the trombone. In the city's public squares, on improvised platforms, there were fable singers, telling a tale chosen from among several by the crowd of artisans, tanners, porters and donkeymen, second-hand clothes dealers, dyers, armorers and the like. To the music of lute or violin, played loud or soft, fast or slow, according to the events that were related, the tale unfolded—and was cut off at a dramatic point, whereupon money would be collected and the audience informed when to return for the next fascinating installment.

Sometimes a musical individual sang himself into trouble. The story goes that a poet, passing by, heard a blacksmith singing his verses all wrong. Entering the shop, the poet threw out the smith's hammer and tongs.

"What the devil are you doing?" cried the blacksmith.

"What are *you?*" cried the poet.

"Following my trade," the smith answered, "and you're ruining my tools."

"Well," said the poet, "if you don't want me to damage your trade, don't damage mine."

6

Making a Living

The Black Death which swept Europe in the fourteenth century destroyed, according to some estimates, a quarter of the population. Uncounted thousands of workers died of this plague. As a result, the survivors were greatly in demand. Thus they were in a position to rebel against unjust laws. Serfs, bound in the Middle Ages to a certain tract of land, began to escape from that near-slavery. Although forbidden by law to do so, thousands stole away from farms to become free laborers in the cities. Many were offered a partnership by the landowners as an inducement to keep on tilling the fields. Nevertheless, the social position of the farmer remained low.

The Man Behind the Plow

In Renaissance Italy almost no one had a good word for the man trudging along back of a plow. It did not matter if he rose at dawn and worked as long as there was light; nor that all Italy depended on the farmer for most of what it ate and drank and wore; nor that more people lived on the land than in the towns.

Townspeople considered the farmer as stupid as the oxen pulling his clumsy plowshare through the hard earth. Writers made him the butt of their jokes: it was said, for instance, that a peasant would faint away if he smelled perfume, and could only be revived by a whiff of manure. On the other hand, the nobles whose land he tilled called him shrewd, cunning—a conniver, always looking out for himself. They said he was a miser. The kindest thing a parish priest could say about the farmer was that he had a hard, stubborn head. An archbishop went farther. He charged the peasants roundabout Florence with misbehaving in church: "They occasionally leap and dance and sing with the women there . . ." Farmers, he said, were given to lying, even under oath. They were all too ready to take the Lord's name in vain. They much preferred arguing in front of the church to going inside and hearing the Mass. Better still, to them, was a drink at the nearest tavern. The archbishop also complained that "very many of them do not confess once in an entire year" and that still fewer took communion. Another charge against the farmers was that they went in for magic rather than prayer and sought to cure themselves and their animals through secret potions and incantations.

Shearing a sheep. Peasants lost employment when owners turned their farms into grazing lands.

If the peasant was dull, it was because drudgery made him so. Actually, the agriculture he practised in Italy was more advanced than that of most European countries. When Charles VIII returned to France from his conquests in Italy at the end of the fifteenth century, the king carried with him a number of gardeners and a man "skilled in the business of breeding fowls."

The Italian peasant also knew how to get out of bondage sooner than most other European serfs. However, serfdom did still exist in the Friuli region (northeast of Venice and near Austria). There, as for hundreds of years, serfs could not leave the land and could be sold like cattle. Actual slavery also existed in the fields of Renaissance Italy. When labor grew scarce—because of plague deaths or the movement of workers into the cities—slaves were imported to help fill the need. Most of them were the victims of war: they were captured soldiers or civilians dragged from their homes. Pope Paul III, at war with England in the early sixteenth century, declared that any English soldiers who were captured could be turned into slaves.

In a worse state than slaves were the so-called "free" laborers who were hired by the day. The owner of a slave had to feed him, give him shelter and keep him clothed. But no one was obliged to do anything for the free laborer. He had two freedoms: the freedom to move about in search of work; and the freedom to starve or become a beggar if he did not find work. He was never far from beggary in any case.

Migrant workers who used to come seasonally to Rome and work in the vineyards could add to their meagre funds in an unusual way: they could dig up treasures left over in the ground from ancient times. They might find medals, agates, cameos, and even jewels such as emeralds, diamonds and rubies. Having no idea of their value, they would part with these treasures for very little. Traders were quick to buy them up, and the objects brought ever higher prices as they passed from hand to hand.

At that time a pair of rough wooden clogs cost the peasant nearly three days of labor. In summer he could solve the problem by going barefoot. In winter, when he needed something between him and the cold, wet or frozen ground, work was scarce and paid a third less, since the day was shorter.

The man who paid out these wages was often not a great deal better off than his hired hand. A bad crop, or brigands driving off his livestock, could put him with the other landless farm workers.

Such a disaster could happen to a peasant who had scratched together enough money to buy his own tools and to rent land. But there was another way of getting ahead for those who were good workers but had almost no money. This system, called *mezzadria* by the Italians, was like our sharecropping. In it the landowner provided all the tools, fertilizer in the form of manure, feed for the farm animals; and he kept the buildings in repair. The peasant sharecropper and his family contributed their labor and farming skills. The peasant also hauled goods for the owner without charge and contributed a fixed number of days of work on the owner's other property. He also had to give the landlord a certain amount of eggs, cheese and chickens, but he could raise and butcher his own pigs. His biggest obligation came at harvest time, when he had to divide the crop with the owner. The grain might be divided half and half, but the peasant could keep a considerably larger share of the wine and olives, which required more hand labor.

Work and scrimp—this was the way a peasant got ahead. A French observer might have been describing the poorer Italian farmers when, at a later date, he described French peasants thus: "Scattered across the countryside you come upon a sort of wild animal. Both male and female, they are black, leaden, burned all over by the sun. They are bound to the earth and they dig at it and move it around with a doggedness that nothing will stop. They make a kind of articulate sound, and when they rise up on their two feet they exhibit a human face. And it turns out they are people."

74

Peasants having their midday meal at harvest time.

Nevertheless, peasant life was not always so gloomy. The Italian farmer, although he knew rain and icy weather, lived in a relatively mild climate. His clothing was at least adequate. We see him with his jet black hair and beard, wearing a white cap, a short black jacket open over a coarse white garment tucked up at the bare thigh, and red stockings rolled just below the knee. His shoes, ankle-high, were pointed and had no heels. He also enjoyed some amusements, mostly drinking at the tavern, watching splendid processions, attending weddings and festivals, dancing and playing games of chance.

He was certainly no worse off than the vigorous, earthy peasants in the pictures of Pieter Bruegel the Elder, a sixteenth-century master in Antwerp's painters' guild. The northern peasants were coarse-featured and had poor teeth. Admittedly, they were not well groomed, but they were well fed and warmly dressed. The women wore aprons, kerchiefs, wide sleeves, skirts of heavy durable cloth. The men wore soft caps of many different shapes, sleeveless jackets over shirts, tight pants (something like the Bavarian and Tyrolean leather knickers still in use today) and thick stockings with seams. Both men and women had sturdy shoes.

75

At a butcher's shop, hand-held scales were used to weigh meat.

Hardly a face showed beauty, but they all appeared gay, hardy and tough. The weaklings generally died off in infancy. The country dancers looked as if they could go on for hours. Knives were rather too much in evidence, the men carrying daggers, or implements looking much like kitchen knives, stuck in their belts. A peasant woman painted by Bruegel—"Mad Meg"—carries a basket and a frying pan, both surprisingly like our own. She, too, has a knife at her belt. Violence was always nearby. An old man, who was born in 1500 and recalled the days of his youth, wrote that everybody carried a weapon then.

The Italian peasant, struggling to get ahead, thought of home only as a place to sleep. In the beginning it was little more than that. He fell at night onto a mattress stuffed with straw. This could be on a floor of packed earth, or possibly on a low, crude wooden platform. His house had few windows and no window glass. Tallow for candles was too expensive, so he lit his hovel with pieces of pitch-filled wood, which gave off a great deal of smoke, or he might place a wick in a dish of olive oil, like the ancient Romans and Greeks.

His wife cooked in clay pots. Later on, a peasant might be able to afford pewter or copper. But the food on the plates was all raised by himself, except the salt fish bought or bartered for at the nearest market. He got along with very few spices but used a good deal of salt—for preserving meat through the lean winter months, but also because he liked his food well salted. Honey was much easier to come by than sugar, so he used it for sweetening. And, just as today, wine was his chief drink.

The Italian peasant moved ahead with the times. Once he had accumulated a small amount of personal property he raised his head out of the dirt. As befitted a man with Roman ancestors, he took to bathing a little more often. That led to wearing underclothes. Then it became a matter of pride, of outdoing his neighbor, to have a decent supply of underwear and tablecloths on the linen shelf. He also began to press his landlord to do more for him. He asked for another ox or cow, pleaded to have his debts paid off, tried to wheedle a dowry for his daughter, kept after the landlord to provide him with a new house and better furniture.

Conditions, of course, varied from place to place, and even in the same area could change overnight. A peasant, like a noble, might be well off one day, a beggar the next. War, the plague, the stars, a spell of evil luck, could make or break him. If his lord's property deeds disappeared, he might become an owner by stubbornly staying where he was and insisting that the land belonged to him.

With every other class against him, the peasant had to look out for himself. At the terrible sack of Rome in 1527 when Spaniards and Germans attacked and gutted the wealthy city, peasants lay in wait beyond the walls to rob the refugees.

Not long after that time, English ambassadors traveling between Vercelli and Pavia found the peasants ruined in their turn. The whole countryside was laid waste. "The most goodly country for

Fruit and vegetables for sale. Italians in particular ate quantities of salads and fruits.

77

wheat and vines that may be seen," they reported, "is so desolate that in all that distance [fifty miles] we saw no man or woman laborers in the field, nor any creature stirring; but in large villages [only] five or six miserable persons; except that in all this distance we saw three women in one place gathering grapes yet upon the vines. . . ."

Working in an orchard. At left, a farmer grafts a branch onto a tree.

Masters and Craftsmen

When it came to classes above the peasant level, Italians had their own way of showing the difference between rich and poor. The prosperous ones were called the "fat people" (*populo grasso*); the commoners were lumped together as the "little people" (*populo minuto*). Among the little people were the masters and workmen in the lesser trades. As in the Middle Ages, a typical woodworker or blacksmith owned his tools, which were few in number, used part of his house for a workshop, displayed his wares there and trained one or more apprentices. The apprentices lived in his house and hoped one day to set up shops of their own. A master took pride in his craftsmanship and earned a good, comfortable living. Beyond that his ambition did not go.

This narrow outlook led to many restrictions. An ordinary man with a desire to rise in the world found himself walled in with rules. Old ways of doing things were always preferred. The man who sold linen could not branch out and sell wool cloth, too. The man who slaughtered pigs could not market the meat at retail. In Venice, the shoemakers' guild was divided into those who made fine shoes and those who made clogs for the ordinary person.

Some of the rules were intended to help the public. To maintain the quality of pewter, which was often cheapened, the maker had to stamp his name on each piece. The price of food was regulated in order to keep the cost of living down. Wool-beaters could not work at night. Because of the drinking and carousing, inns were not allowed close to churches. All this was good, but the total effect of so many regulations was to put a brake on the ambitious. If, for example, you sold old clothes you could not also sell new coats.

Slaughtering time. Pork was enjoyed although it was thought by some to cause leprosy.

These rules were not suited to a society that was on the move—and Europe was now moving forward. Especially in the northern half of Italy everyone seemed to want to do something constructive: paint, carve, open a shop, weave a finer cloth, write, sail a ship into the unknown, build a church, plan a city. Actually, much of this was only a wishful dream, because only a few created masterpieces or made fortunes or discovered new lands. But the few were enough to start others toward new and shining goals.

In Florence the spirit of activity led to an attempt to eliminate idleness. The belief was that each person should contribute to the society in which he lived. Some parents even made wills asking the government to fine any son of theirs who refused to engage in a regular profession. One law made a non-worker a non-citizen. Any male of sixteen and over who was not enrolled in a guild—that is, a trade or professional association—could not officially be a Florentine. There was, incidentally, a guild for every useful occupation, from practicing medicine to laying bricks. Anyone who insisted on

The gentry visit a farmer's kitchen. Behind them, their maid looks haughtily about.

Above left:
A silk weaver at work.

Above right:
A tailor's shop.

remaining idle was called a *scioperato*, or ne'er-do-well. His family lost standing in the community and could be fined. He himself might be thrown in jail or be placed in the stocks to be jeered at by passersby and pelted with garbage. Idleness among those who worked was also discouraged. Cosimo I, the dictator of Florence when that city ceased to be a republic, ruled that any servant found loitering in the streets after the evening bell had rung would have his right hand cut off.

Even religion was called upon to help further production. Each morning in a certain church monks celebrated Mass for the benefit of those who belonged to the wool-finishers guild and prayed for the guild's prosperity. In their turn, the guilds built many chapels and tried to encourage moral conduct. Betting and games of chance were forbidden on woolen guild property. Tale-bearing, gossip and the stirring up of quarrels were severely punished. In the silk guild, two inspectors checked the moral behavior of workers as well as their skill and willingness to work.

Guilds were civic-minded, too. Some of them bore the cost of city improvements that nowadays are financed out of public funds. A guild might have a street paved, or sewers dug, or establish a school or hospital. Guilds commissioned expensive paintings and sculpture. Some of them provided homes for members who had grown too old or sick to work.

Surprisingly, the guilds' civic functions occasionally included such petty duties as seeing that no diseased animals drank at public fountains or that boys did not spin tops in the street. Such restrictions were nothing compared to those imposed on workers. Employees of the silk guild in Florence could go out of the city only with a special permit and for urgent reasons. No worker would have dreamed of trying to win an eight-hour day. Work began at dawn and ended when the light failed, which meant many a fifteen-hour day in summer. There was a half-hour pause for breakfast around ten o'clock and a longer pause for another meal around five in the afternoon. Compensating somewhat for the long hours were frequent church holidays—forty or more a year, not counting Sundays. And employees, then as now, added some holidays of their own.

Coming of the Factory System

Despite such occasional independence, the average worker in wool and silk was already caught in the beginnings of the factory system. Where the guild of a trade had once protected the individual worker, and enabled him to advance and become the master-owner of a small shop, it now stood in his way. What happened was that a city, for example Florence, would come to excel in a given trade. The clothmakers of Florence could buy raw wool in the British Isles, bring it to Florence, turn it into cloth, ship the cloth back to England, and still compete with British weavers in their own market. This could be done only by men operating on a large scale and with plenty of money. A group of strong men found ways to control the wool-makers guild: they admitted members of their own families, thus insuring control from one generation to the next. This practice also created a large pool of skilled workers who could either work for the managers at fixed wages, or starve. Nor could these workers

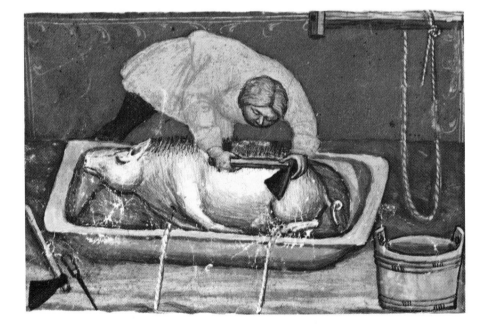

Scraping the bristles from a butchered hog.

Right:
Two methods are used in pressing grapes for wine: bare feet and a wooden press.

improve their position by setting up a loom and weaving cloth at home, for this was strictly forbidden.

On the other hand, the guild leaders encouraged women to spin wool into yarn by hand and at home because this provided plenty of cheap labor. The women were of course not organized and had to accept whatever they were offered or they lost the work.

As their trade expanded, clothmakers turned more and more toward modern factory methods. The new system was so much more productive than work at home that a silk mill in Bologna run by water power produced as much as did four thousand women using the old hand methods. Nearly a century after this, in 1435, a traveler reported that Bologna had a hundred mill races, that is, streams diverted from the river Reno to turn water wheels. These wheels provided power not only for the silk mills but also for those that ground wheat and spices, sawed wood, made paper, and polished armor.

Unfortunately, something more was lost through the new methods than the jobs of four thousand women. The workers themselves began to be looked upon as machines. In the small shops that had formerly worked up silk thread, women sat before a long trough heated by a wood fire. The cocoons of the silkworm were brought to this trough by other women who carried them on their heads in wide, shallow baskets. Into such a shop, with doors open on the street, women friends of the workers could drop in for a chat, bringing their babies. The life of the town passed by. This easy-going atmosphere contrasted with the later condition of the woolen workers in Florence.

The old comradely days of master, journeymen and apprentices working together in a small shop were gone. A journeyman was now only a wage-earner. Not only could he be fired at any time, but he had practically no hope of becoming a master. The new equipment cost more than he would ever earn. Besides, the right to be a master was now handed down from father to son, and the proportion of masters was rapidly falling off. As early as the middle of the fourteenth century a scant two hundred Florentine owners employed thirty thousand workmen. The steadily decreasing number of owners fixed prices and set wage rates to suit themselves. They used the government to make laws that would keep the workers in their place. Workers who had fallen into debt could not change their jobs until the debts were paid, so that a man who owed money virtually became a slave. To force wages down, foreigners were brought in and kept in ghettos. This prevented them from mixing with the Florentines and finding out how badly they were being exploited. As a result of these policies, unemployment rose until

Merchants selling pewter, ornaments and shoes.

Florence at one time had 22,000 beggars. Those who did find jobs were called to work by a bell. Hard-driving foremen pushed the men to produce more and more. A man who left before his work was finished could be taken out and publicly whipped.

Thus the Renaissance in Italy marked the end of the golden days of the guilds. Wool-combers might still appear before the Doge crowned with olive leaves, and weavers might appear in long scarves of silver cloth, but they were already a part, although they did not know it, of the drab Industrial Revolution of the future.

Little Pawnbrokers and Big Bankers

To finance industry on the new, larger scale there had to be huge sums of money. Churchmen in the Middle Ages had cautioned mankind against money, saying that the love of it was the root of all evil. "Gold is the father of joy and the son of sorrow," a motto read; "who lacks it grieves, and who has it trembles." The taking

85

of interest on money was forbidden by the Church. Nevertheless, there had to be money available, and such a great business center as Florence during the Renaissance had three classes of banks: pawn-shops, "little banks," and "big banks," all of which charged interest in one form or another.

The emblem of a pawnshop was a length of red cloth at the door. People would bring in their clothing, hand tools, jewelry and other possessions, and borrow money on them, much as they do today. Although classed as a banker, a pawnbroker was not allowed to join the bankers guild. He was fined a fixed amount each year for charging interest; and the Church barred him from receiving communion or having last rites said over him.

Franciscan monks tried to save the poor from the excessive charges of the pawnbrokers. They set up agencies called *monti di pietà*, meaning "mounts of mercy," for lending money to the needy but without interest. However, the monks found that it was quite expensive to run them; so the Church permitted an extra sum to be charged on a loan.

A farm woman offers a rooster for sale.

*Right:
Builders chisel stone, carry mortar, and use an early version of a crane.*

The "little banks" avoided the problem of interest by hiding their charges. Like many modern merchants, they sold goods on the installment plan and simply included the interest in the selling price. They seem to have dealt mainly in jewelry.

Above the "little banks" were the "big banks," the *banchi grossi*. They usually had rather modest beginnings. At the start of the fifteenth century the important Medici bank had a staff of only five in its Florence headquarters, and a total of seventeen employees for the whole of Italy. Yet they carried on banking operations all over Europe. Moreover, they bought and sold goods on their own account, and acted as agents for other merchants.

In addition to their regular business, banks carried out a variety of odd commissions: they had representatives look through monastery libraries for books by classical authors. They ordered tapestries to be woven in special designs for rich customers. They even acted as talent scouts, and sought out choir boys with exceptional voices. All this they accomplished not only with a very small staff but without calculating machines. To do their figuring, even for sums in the hundreds of thousands, they used an abacus.

In Germany, a well-known family, the Fuggers of Augsburg, became leading bankers of the fifteenth and sixteenth centuries. Jacob Fugger had seven sons who greatly increased the family wealth. Wishing to help the poor, Jacob developed an early form of low cost housing, putting up dwellings which he rented for a trifling sum.

Fifteenth-century French carpenters using an auger to bore holes and an adze to shape wood.

Above left:
Glass blowing.

Above right:
At a sugar factory in
Florence, the man in the
foreground is chopping up
sugar cane. At right are
finished sugar loaves.

In the beginning, the banker was chiefly a money-changer who sat back of a cloth-covered bench (the word "bank" is said to come from this bench) with his account book and various currencies laid out on the bench. As European trade grew larger and more complicated, the business of changing money became less important than lending it or transferring it from place to place. Nevertheless, the Renaissance bank retained its early simplicity. The bench was replaced by a counter; a few tables and the useful abacus were added, but the staff remained small. In Florence, London, Lübeck, Paris and Bruges, plain offices like this enabled international trade to develop on a large scale. Through them men became rich enough to buy the palaces, paintings, rich vessels, cloth of gold and silver, jewels, tapestries and statues that we think of as typically "Renaissance."

The Paper That Was Safer Than Money

One of the most valuable devices used by these bankers was called a "bill of exchange." Instead of having to carry money along bandit-infested roads or across stormy seas, a man could give his banker the money and tell him to whom it should be paid in another country. The banker would usually arrange to have the money paid to his agent abroad, or to a merchant from whom the depositor was buying foreign goods. Since transactions of this kind were going on all the time and in all directions, bankers could balance an out-

going bill of exchange against an incoming one. Thus a great deal of business could be done by means of these bills of exchange without moving very much gold coin from one place to another. To make this transfer of money still easier, banks set up branches in foreign countries. Soon the Florentine banks were doing such a large volume of business in buying, selling, lending and transferring money that Florence came to be called "the fountain of gold."

The person who contributed most to this volume of business was the Pope. He was the banks' biggest customer, for he received sums

A banker's wife looks on as he weighs gold coins on delicate scales.

of money from the faithful all over the western world. No one could transfer these funds more quickly or safely than the Florentine banks with their network of branches. This business involved a contradictory attitude toward the Church: on the one hand the banks sought her business; on the other, they disobeyed her command that no money should be lent out at interest. Lenders got around this prohibition in a number of ways. A noble borrowed money and repaid the exact sum, but added a costly jewel as a "gift." Or a man might receive one thousand florins but see the loan written down in the bank's books as twelve hundred florins and know that this was the sum he must repay. No matter what method was used to disguise the fact, all banks charged interest on loans, often at very high rates. It was a popular saying in Florence that twenty-five percent interest amounted to nothing, fifty percent would do to pass the time, while one hundred percent might prove interesting. Florentine bankers thought one fourteenth-century English king so bad a risk that they put his rate up to 260 percent. King Edward III got his revenge by refusing to pay either principal or interest on his loans. He was so deeply in debt to Florence's bankers—"a whole kingdom's worth," said one shareholder—that on his refusal to pay his debts, the greatest bank in Florence failed, and was followed shortly by the second largest.

Going bankrupt was only one of the ways in which Renaissance businessmen resembled modern ones. Many other practices of the time were so advanced that they are still used five centuries later. The Italian banks invented the partnership; and some of them had boards of directors. Like modern accountants, they used double-entry bookkeeping; and they invested in other kinds of businesses and superintended their management. And, as we have seen, they established foreign branches and introduced the bill of exchange.

Checks were also used, but to a limited extent. Most clients preferred the older method of going to the bank and telling the clerk to transfer a certain sum to some individual or firm. It seems strange to us that they would consider this safer than writing a check. The reason for this was that bankers and merchants did not trust a signature as sole means of identification. It was not enough for a responsible official to sign important papers. Instead, a special bank officer wrote the entire document in his own hand. When the document arrived, the recipient would bring out a sample that he had on file and check the two scripts to see if they had been written by the same man. This system, although clumsy, reduced the risk of forgery.

The Wonder of Learning

7

As we have seen, the Renaissance was an explosion of interest in human learning, in the knowledge of this world rather than the next. Although men still remained devout believers, they turned from religious studies to "human" ones. They became "humanists." And one of the main reasons for this great outburst of learning was the invention, in the fifteenth century, of printing.

Up to this time all books had been hand-written copies which took a long time to produce. Some of these manuscripts were exquisite works of art. In one great lady's collection there was a book of poems written on white damask and embroidered with diamonds. Some libraries had Persian books with characters in glossy black ink on silky paper powdered with gold or silver dust. The first two leaves were usually illuminated—that is, "brightened" or hand-painted—and the whole manuscript might be perfumed with essence of roses. But the average citizen, even if he was able to read, could not afford such manuscripts. Now came the invention (around 1436 or 1437), by Johann Gutenberg, a German, of printing from movable metal type. This made it possible for the first time to print, quickly and easily, copy after copy of a book.

The Miracle of the Printed Book

Books flooded the world, changing everything. "My library was dukedom enough," says a character in Shakespeare. Some, however, at first disapproved of the new, printed books. The owners of hand-written books, realizing that they would be losing their advantage over the common people, still hoarded their knowledge and did not wish to see it spread to the "common herd." Isabella d'Este, the First Lady of Mantua, asked a writer to be sure to send her his works "before they were printed."

One of the earliest of printed books was the Gutenberg Bible. It was not produced by Gutenberg himself. He ran into financial difficulties, and his creditors took over his equipment in 1445. It was they who printed his Bible. The so-called Father of Printing, like many inventors, died in poverty.

Meanwhile university students kept on making their own texts by writing down what their instructor read from his book. When he paused to comment on a passage, they would add this information

A printing shop.

as well. Those who took dictation accurately got the best versions. There must have been many such books, for students from all over Europe, eager to acquire the "new learning," were flocking to the universities.

Student Life

Italian institutions of higher learning were especially popular. These universities were organized almost haphazardly. Their student bodies ranged from boys in their early teens to men of thirty, and their quarters were quite unlike a modern campus. Often a university owned no buildings at all, and if its faculty became annoyed with the townspeople they might move the school elsewhere. Even the renowned University of Padua held classes in whatever rooms it could find throughout the city. Not until 1493, almost three centuries

93

after its founding, did it acquire a home of its own. Then nearby Venice gave it an old palace that had been turned into an inn called "At the Sign of the Bull."

Students varied greatly in their qualifications. The best prepared had had private tutors, whom they sometimes brought along to the university together with a private secretary. Others had gone to church schools, for better or worse; many teaching priests hardly knew enough Latin to get through a Mass, while many a schoolmaster was a teacher only because he needed the money. To improve elementary education, Italian cities set up their own public schools. Theoretically, the children of any citizen could attend; actually, most students came from the more prosperous families. Working parents saw no need for their sons to know more than they themselves did, unless the sons were going into a trade where reading, writing and arithmetic were almost essential. There were uneducated stonecarvers who simply copied an inscription letter by letter without understanding a word of it.

In Venice, only those who proved they were both educated and respectable were allowed to teach in the public schools. As in medieval schools, teachers kept order by frequent and often brutal floggings. Even small children were beaten: a sixteenth-century speller shows a young pupil held like a sack on the back of an older child, so the master could strike him with a doubled strap.

Venetian children from seven to ten were taught to read and write in Latin, and then took up logic, rhetoric and poetry. From fourteen to eighteen they studied music, arithmetic, geometry and astronomy. Little of this was of use to a youth who would have to earn his own living as soon as he left school. Its purpose was twofold: to instil culture for its own sake, and to prepare students for the university. University courses were given in Latin, which all educated people knew. Even business needed this universal tongue, since contracts were written in Latin. By means of it, knowledge moved easily from country to country.

Students had some eighty European universities to choose from, but almost none of these had a student body of as much as one thousand. The popular University of Padua enrolled 1,210 in 1561, and averaged six hundred during the next four years. Students were restless; when a favorite professor moved, his classes often followed him to the next post. This made it quite simple to start a new university. The would-be founder had only to secure a building and hire some popular teachers; these would bring a student body along with them. Nor did the school need a large staff. Luring a professor to another institution was easy enough, for the teachers preferred a wandering

Despite the confusion around him, a young noble pays close attention to his teacher.

94

life. In one case, Florence was so anxious to retain a certain professor of law who had packed up and was leaving for the University of Padua that the city jailed him. Top university professors earned surprisingly large salaries. Where a bank manager might receive less than two hundred florins (about eight hundred dollars) a year, Padua was willing to pay a thousand florins for a teacher of law—this at a time when teaching below the university level was badly paid, and an aristocrat might teach for nothing in order to show off his learning. Professors taught about four hours in the morning, stopped at ten for lunch, then taught another four hours in the afternoon and sometimes after supper at five. Students were expected to study until bedtime.

In England, except for the nobility, who did as they pleased and were treated respectfully even by teachers, the average scholar had a harder time than the Italians. But then, his life had been equally

Pope Sixtus IV visits the Vatican Library, which he helped to found.

hard in secondary school: he was used to long hours, strict discipline, poor food and cold rooms. At Cambridge University some rose at four o'clock, others at five. After communal prayers, a sermon, lectures and study, a thin lunch was served at ten. Work in the afternoon was much as in Italy, and the evening meal was also at five. More or less nourished, the students then toiled over their notes in unheated quarters until nine or ten. Most of the year they were so chilled by this time that they spent a half hour walking about or running to warm up their feet.

To England's credit, quite a number of poor youths managed to get a university training. Some were sent by wealthy men who wanted to give a bright boy his chance. Others spent their summers working or begging, the latter not so frowned on as it is today. An impoverished student might travel about, offering prayers in exchange for charity.

In Italy anyone could attend the University of Florence regardless of age, class or finances if he was a registered Florentine citizen of legitimate birth. He received one gold florin, about four dollars, a month. Medical students also had an allowance of red wine and spices "to keep up their spirits." In Venice, too, there were no class distinctions at the university and private charity housed the deserving. Mantua's famous educator, Vittorino da Feltre, supported as many as seventy boys from working class families at his school for children, called the Joyous House. It stood on a lake shore and had frescoed walls and avenues of plane trees and acacias. He taught boys and girls together, giving them simple food and encouraging sports and games. Besides the curriculum, which included Latin, Greek, mathematics, grammar, logic, philosophy, singing and dancing, he taught

An arithmetic book, with multiplication tables at left, and, at right, a table showing how to change Florentine money.

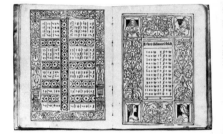

A schoolmaster and his wife teaching and disciplining children.

lessons in character. Swearing was forbidden; lying was the worst crime; good manners were essential. Vittorino set an example himself, living modestly, wearing sandals and the same clothes in all seasons. He was so revered that one noble, a marquis, never sat down in his presence.

Besides the subjects taught by Vittorino, there were exciting new developments for Renaissance students to learn about. Higher mathematics embodied advances in trigonometry and algebra. The use of decimal fractions and decimal weights and measures began to be promoted in Europe. Nicholas Copernicus expounded his system of astronomy. The Copernican system, called the "sun-centered" (or heliocentric) theory of the universe, demonstrated that our earth and the other planets move around the sun—not the sun around the earth, as people in the Middle Ages had believed. More was now discovered about geography, and there were better maps. Chemistry and physics went forward. Scientists of various countries furthered the knowledge of botany. Animals and minerals were also studied. As they progressed, students could join secret clubs of scientists, where new ideas might be debated, safe from interference by the church.

An English visitor to Italy in the early sixteenth century commented with snobbish approval that more university students there belonged to the upper classes. He noted their sober dress and good table manners. Roman students were forbidden to wear "noble" cloth, the finely finished cloth that was a specialty of Florence. On state occasions they were permitted to don scarlet gowns trimmed with gold embroidery and rich fur.

Italian students lived well enough. The very wealthy usually came to have a good time, and their tutors and secretaries kept them from failing their courses, while they themselves staged balls in their rented palaces, jousted, gambled and ran after girls. Gentlemen-students who were more interested in learning could live in elegant boarding-houses—*pensioni*—where a guest paid seven gold florins a month for himself and six for his valet. Cheaper boarding houses were available, too, and professors, such as the famous astronomer Galileo, would take serious students into their homes.

Along with easier living conditions, Italian students enjoyed considerable freedom. There was some self-government. They elected from among themselves a rector who ruled on disputes and maintained order. At Bologna the law students hired their own professors. In general, students could simply drop a professor they did not like.

When it came to amusements, students met with many a "No." Cock-fights, bull-baiting, gambling, even dancing, games and dining out, might be forbidden. One reason for this was the fights they were

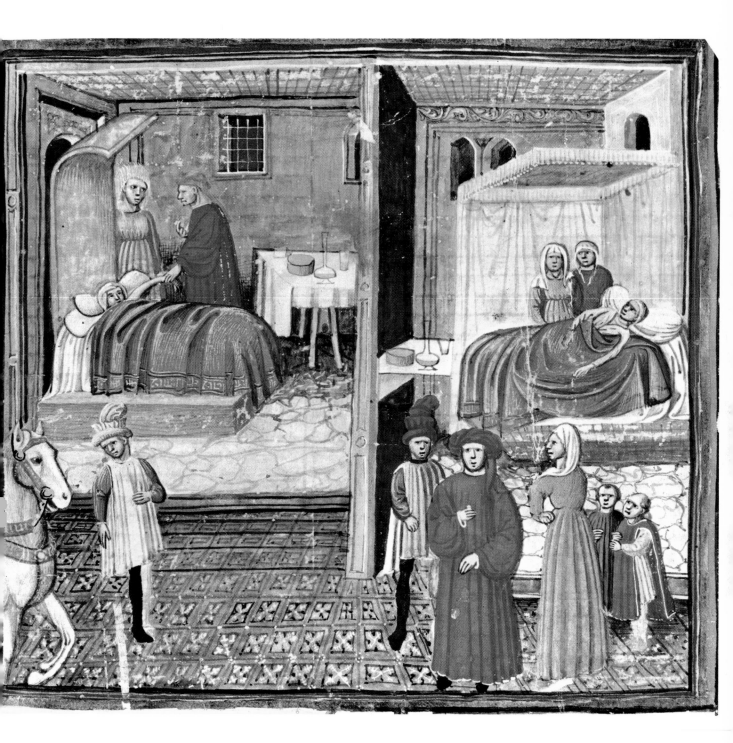

apt to get into when out on the town. Townspeople resented the students' superior ways, while the students suspected tavern-keepers and merchants of cheating them. Riots between "town and gown" —the students wore long black gowns—were a feature of university life. Besides these there were battles between the different schools of a university or different groups of foreign students. Thus, Germans at Padua drank beer together, took military drill under their own instructors, established a library and engaged in occasional duels among themselves. It was dangerous to oppose such an organization.

A doctor visits a sick person and, at left, takes a patient's pulse.

99

Medicine, Strange Cures and Quackery

Among all the subjects studied at a university, medicine, perhaps, showed the greatest advance. True, medicine still had one foot in the Middle Ages. Newer surgery and a better understanding of the human body were available, but many doctors held to old methods and remedies. Some cast their eyes heavenward in treating a disease, not in prayer but because they believed, along with astrologers, that every part of the body was governed by a planet. A doctor of that time might, for example, refuse to bleed a patient unless the moon was in its second quarter.

Bleeding was a favorite cure-all, and even those near death might be diligently bled. Doctors opened a vein to let out "bad blood,"

A professor lecturing at a university. He has put one student to sleep.

or placed live leeches—as many as twenty at a time—on the patient to suck blood out. One treatment for madness included the taking of enough blood from a vein in the forehead to fill an eggshell. Insanity was a distressing ailment, then as now, but apparently did not make a man unfit for office; the chief officer of Castle St. Angelo, the Pope's stronghold in Rome, was intermittently mad, and so, for many years, was the reigning King of France.

People attributed healing powers to products that cost a great deal or came from far away. Thus pepper, ginger and other spices from the East were highly valued as medicines, and tobacco, newly discovered in America, found favor as a pain reducer. Sugar, a luxury, was believed to be a cure for lung congestion and was sometimes flavored with violets. Gold, taken internally, was supposed to arrest or at least to conceal leprosy.

Health hazards included birth. Many an infant and many a mother did not survive. Smallpox was also a great danger. Indeed, there was a saying that mothers counted their children only after they had had this disease. Wounds were an everyday affair. Ague, "the stone," that is, kidney and gall stones, gout, and various fevers were common. Bubonic plague was always erupting locally and changing everyone's plans, either for the moment or forever.

Although we do not always know why, many strange cures of the time were effective. A wound might be treated with wormwood which had been thrown on a red hot tile and soaked in Greek wine. Bacon fat was rubbed into bruises. Open sores were plugged with lint and covered with a plaster. Doctors prescribed perfumes, powdered pearls, laxatives, lotions and unctions. One eye remedy was fleur-de-lis, including the entire plant, simmered over a slow fire. Borax and also white lead were recommended for pimples, and breath was sweetened with cardamon or licorice. Boiled toad was not unknown for heart disease, and, indeed, modern science has shown that a toad's skin contains something like the heart drug, digitalis. Worms were considered good for fevers. Even more bizarre were such cures as suspending a patient upside down, or preventing him from falling asleep.

So far as the healing arts were concerned, the superstitions of the past held the doctors back. They believed that the body was made of four elements: earth, air, fire and water. From these elements came four "humors": blood, phlegm, yellow bile and black bile. The amount and purity of these four humors in the body determined one's disposition and health. A man who had too much black bile was melancholy. If he had too much phlegm he was phlegmatic.

The selfishness of doctors also hindered the progress of medicine. A doctor who discovered a new remedy or successfully used a new operation often tried to keep the discovery to himself. A man hugged his knowledge to his bosom, or kept it in his family, which is one reason why there tended to be families of doctors.

Despite such backward attitudes and superstitions, the science of medicine did advance. Nature began to be referred to as a healer, and the study of medicinal herbs was widespread. The first printed book of such herbs came out in 1484, describing 150 different plants, and before the middle of the sixteenth century Pisa and Padua had botanical gardens for use in teaching medicine. Another school of healing relied on chemicals and a long war between mineralists and herbalists began. A noted Swiss doctor, Paracelsus, wandering about in search of knowledge, did not hesitate to collect medical information from barbers and executioners, bath-keepers, gypsies, midwives and fortune-tellers.

When it came to medicine, Italian universities led the field. The English scientist William Harvey may well have been guided toward his great discovery of the circulation of the blood by what he learned from Fabrizio, his Italian professor. This man had noted a significant fact about the valves of the veins—that their mouths were all in the direction of the heart. Fabrizio did not carry his observation further, but he did other valuable work, especially in the study of unborn infants, and wrote the first illustrated book in this field.

In 1546, some seventy years before Harvey, the Italian Fracastoro set forth a theory that could have been of vital importance to the study of disease. He believed that disease was carried from one person to another by means of extremely small bodies that increased in number in the infected person. With the imperfect scientific equipment of Fracastoro's day, this remained only a theory but it did foreshadow the modern study of bacteria. People certainly knew that touching a sick person had something to do with catching his ailment. In plague time they would call out to one another: "Let us keep our distance!" Many shops would close, and if money was paid out, it would be received in a tray, not by hand.

Early Surgery

Renaissance medicine owed most of its true progress to the revived interest in anatomy and in the human body. Corpses could be cut open and studied in all the medical schools of Italy; otherwise, Harvey could never have made his revolutionary discovery. But bodies for dissection were scarce. Some came from hospitals or from the gallows and occasionally a corpse would disappear from a

A bespectacled chemist supervises the workers in his laboratory.

IOÁNES
STRATENSÍS
FLANDRVS
1570

cemetery. The bodies of criminals who died in prison might be taken to the dissection table if no relatives or friends intervened. The demand was great, particularly at Bologna, where one professor of anatomy cut up and examined a hundred cadavers. Leonardo da Vinci gained a detailed knowledge of the human body by dissecting more than thirty cadavers.

Besides increasing man's knowledge of how the different organs are affected by disease, all this study of the human structure enabled surgeons to improve their techniques and to invent new instruments. An Italian and a Frenchman both devised new ways of tying up arteries and veins, thus making operations safer than before. New surgical tools such as the trocar and the cannula, used respectively for exploration and drainage, appeared.

So informal was medical practice that one instrument was invented in mid-operation. A leading surgeon, with implements of coarse steel, was clumsily removing infected sections of a girl's finger bones; a goldsmith who was watching the proceedings begged the doctor to wait. He ran to his shop, and soon was back with "a little scalping-iron of steel, extremely thin and curved" which "cut like a razor." The operation was a complete success.

Even blood transfusion was tried. When Pope Innocent VIII lay dying, a doctor proposed introducing the blood of a ten-year-old boy into the Pontiff's veins. Attempts were made with three different boys, but the Pope was not revived and all the boys died.

Plastic surgeons had better luck. They repaired facial injuries with

An anatomy lesson.

104

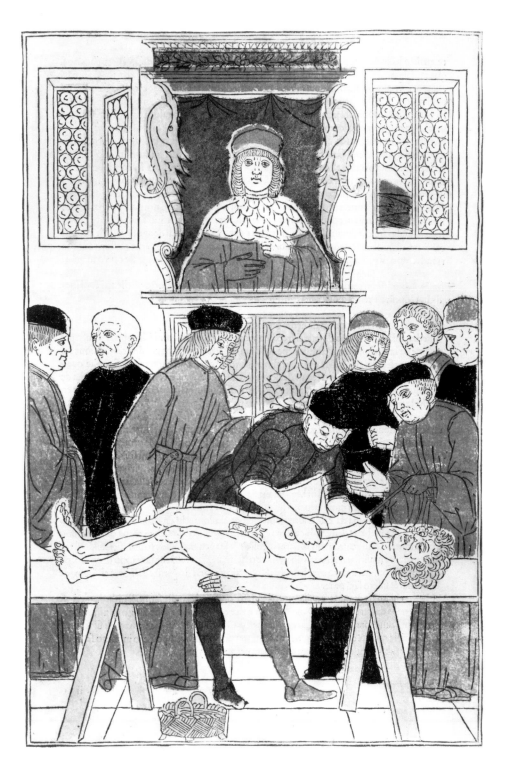

Two kinds of surgeons. Directed by a "long-robe" surgeon above him, a "short-robe" surgeon performs the actual dissection.

skin grafts taken from other parts of the patient's body, becoming so skilful that only faint lines showed where the edges of skin had been joined. Here was another "re-birth," since the art of plastic surgery had been practiced in ancient times but lost for centuries.

Italian hospitals were the marvels of Europe. For one thing, they were exceptionally clean. They were also, in many cases, beautiful. Famous architects designed some of them and painters had their

105

works hung in them. Martin Luther, the famous reformer, who visited Italy while still a priest, found the hospital system one of the few things he could praise. He spoke of the good food, and of "careful attendants and learned physicians." He told of the exact procedure when a patient entered the hospital: ". . . his clothes are removed in the presence of a notary who makes a faithful inventory of them, and they are kept safely. A white smock is put on him, and he is laid on a comfortable bed, with clean linen. Presently two doctors come to him, and servants bring him food in clean vessels."

Luther also told of how ladies of good family took turns as nurses. They stayed at the hospital for a few days, wearing a veil the entire time so that no one might learn who they were. As one completed her tour of duty, another took her place. All this shows a marked advance over the three basic kinds of hospitals in the Middle Ages— the leper hospitals, almshouses for old and infirm poor, and nursing homes with indifferent attendants and no resident doctor.

A hazard that faced doctors themselves was to be entrusted with too important a patient. A famous doctor, brought in to treat Lorenzo the Magnificent, leading member of the powerful Medici family of Florence, was unable to save him. When the doctor's body was later discovered in a well, some thought he had committed suicide over his failure, but the more cynical decided he had been thrown there.

Few believed in doctors completely. Sometimes a contract would be drawn up whereby the physician would receive no pay unless he cured a given ailment. City authorities tried hard to weed out quacks. Venice required doctors to swear that they would not delay a patient's recovery in order to collect a larger fee. No one was allowed to practice medicine in Venice unless he had completed a four-year course in a medical school. Physicians and surgeons were required to take a refresher course in anatomy at least once a year, and a later law obliged them to meet together and discuss cases every month.

Prescription druggists also came in for close supervision, as well they might, since they had many opportunities to substitute a cheap ingredient for a costly one. The government set a limit on how much could be charged for a prescription. Doctors were supposed to check on the accuracy with which their prescriptions were filled, and were forbidden to accept money from the druggist for sending business his way. An inspector came around regularly to check the files and observe the druggist in operation.

In those days, as now, druggists sold a variety of goods. Besides ointments, syrups and plasters of various kinds, they carried all manner of spices, as well as writing paper, candy, and even jewelry

The martyrdom of the monk Savonarola at Florence. Huge crowds, not shown here, watched the execution of this great reformer.

and varnish. In addition they had another sideline: they would sell the prescriptions of an especially able physician to other less skilled practitioners.

The surgeons of that day were divided into two classes: the "long robes" and the "short robes." The former had been to medical school and had learned current theories of treatment and procedure. They did not like to soil their long robes with blood and left the actual operating to barbers, executioners, and men like Ambroise Paré, an army doctor who is called the "father of French surgery." These surgeons wore short robes. There was still another kind of surgeon, but his work was scarcely professional. He was a migrant, travelling from place to place, operating and leaving town at once—which may be where we get the phrase "to cut and run."

Alchemy and Witchcraft

Allied to medicine was another branch of learning, alchemy, an early kind of chemistry. Essentially, alchemy was the supposed art of changing baser metals to gold and silver by means of a magical stone or substance called the "Philosophers' Stone." At the same time, alchemists looked for a cure-all which would keep a man's earthly life going forever. This "elixir of life" was also a magical potion or powder that had to do with gold, for it was thought that drinkable gold might prove to be a universal cure. As we have seen, gold was believed useful in the treatment of leprosy. Leading scientists believed in the fundamentals of alchemy until well into the eighteenth century.

In spite of the wonderful new learning, most of the people in Renaissance times were still woefully ignorant and believed in all kinds of delusions and superstitions. To them a special ring could make its wearer invisible or give him two bodies at once. A ship's captain could buy a favorable wind. An alchemist named Peter d'Apono had seven spirits in seven glass bottles, well corked so that none could escape. Just as in the Middle Ages, there were many who made much of the power of the devil and thought that anyone who acted strangely was a witch, or had made a pact with Satan. The Renaissance "knew" and proved by "confessions" taken down at first hand that a person could be in touch with the devil, sign a hell-pact and do demonic works. Witches and warlocks (men and women thought to be in league with the devil) were supposed to be able to make cattle sick, blight crops, and prevent women from having children.

The monk San Bernardino preaching to a great crowd in which the men are separated from the women by a barrier.

108

It was already legal to burn heretics, that is, those who criticized the church, and from the fourteenth century on, heresy and witchcraft were lumped together, both being considered of the devil. Thousands of innocent persons were put to death on this account. Women were particularly suspect: being the "weaker vessel," woman was easier for the devil to corrupt. Although witches had been ignored for long periods, they were savagely persecuted from the fifteenth century until well into the eighteenth. The Parliament of Paris did not stop the persecution of witchcraft until 1660; and Europe's last legal witch-burning took place in Poland in 1793.

Rebels in the Church: the Reformation

As we have seen, the Renaissance was a shift from the medieval tendency to ignore this world, to a concentration on worldly things and especially money and pleasure. Christ was a carpenter's son who said, "My kingdom is not of this world." His leading apostle was a humble fisherman. Yet their successors, the Popes and higher clergy of the Renaissance, were haughty princes, richer than some kings. They competed with other rulers, often oppressed the poor, and forgot the example of purity and love that Christ had set. Their self-indulgence, their corrupt love of luxury caused a violent reaction: reformers appeared who cried out for a return to the simple religion and plain living of Christ and the apostles.

It is a mistake to think that the German reformer Martin Luther alone started the sixteenth-century reform movement known as the Reformation. But Luther set ablaze a long-smouldering fire of indignation. After Luther, Protestant sects began to spring up all over northern Europe. And although these groups split up into many branches, virtually all were united on two things: Bible reading and purity of life.

In the Middle Ages, ordinary people were not supposed to read the Bible, and indeed it had not been translated out of Hebrew, Greek and Latin into such local languages as English and French. The main goal of the reformers, however, was to "arm the simple layman with Scripture." A literary monument of the later Renaissance, England's King James Bible, completed in 1611, was the work of great scholars who humbly wrote: "We are poor instruments to make God's holy Truth to be yet more and more known unto the people. . . ." Unlike the Middle Ages, the Renaissance placed an increasing emphasis on the importance of the common man.

Following the Reformation, worshippers received both wine and wafers at communion.

Burning the Vanities

There were, broadly speaking, two kinds of reformers in the Renaissance. One attacked the corruption of manners and morals typical of the age. Such men drew thousands of people with their eloquence, their sincerity, and—because there were no voice amplifiers—their necessarily loud voices. One of these was Friar Conecte, who dared to condemn the enormous headdresses, known as hennins, worn by many women of fashion. Normally the chief burghers of Flanders and Northern France would have a scaffold erected in the largest square when this popular preacher was to speak, and as many as twenty thousand might assemble to hear themselves denounced.

We read that Friar Conecte greatly blamed "the noble ladies, and all others who dressed their heads in so ridiculous a manner, and who expended such sums on the luxuries of apparel. He was so vehement against them that no woman thus dressed dared to appear in his presence." The Friar mobilized gangs of boys to run after fashionable ladies and utter rude cries about their hennins. The fine ladies took to caps, at least while Friar Conecte was in town. But, says the chronicler, "this reform did not last long, for just as snails, when anyone passes by them, draw in their horns, and then when all danger seems over, put them forth again, so these ladies, shortly after the preacher had quit their country . . . began to resume their huge headdresses, and wore them even higher than before." At the close of each sermon, the Friar would ask for backgammon boards, chess boards, ninepins, and all other "vanities" including hennins, to be brought to his raised platform, would have a bonfire lit in the square before him, and throw all these "luxuries" into the flames. Unfortunately he was later charged with heresy, and he himself, publicly in Rome, had to follow the people's frivolous toys and absurd feminine headgear into the fire.

Of far greater stature, but still a reformer of morals, was Florence's Savonarola. For a brief time this ailing monk with the beaklike nose and dark, smouldering eyes ruled Florence. He organized groups of children, dressed them in white, cut their hair short and crowned them with flowers or olive leaves. Thousands of them would walk in processions, singing hymns as they went. People flocked to church to hear the childrens' choirs. Savonarola, too, had a bonfire to burn vanities, such as indecent pictures and carnival masks, which the children collected from door to door. "My doctrine is the doctrine of godly living!" he cried. He denounced the corruption of men in high office and told the people that God's judgment was at hand. He was, therefore, also attacked by the leaders. The Florentines, terrified that the Pope would excommunicate them and then their trade would be cut off, rose against the reformer, tortured him, hanged him and burned his dead body.

The other type of reformer wished to make changes not only in morals but in the doctrines of the church. These were the "Protestants," men like Martin Luther who, as we have seen, went back to the Bible and other ancient books and asked themselves and one another what they really believed.

To the Renaissance man-in-the-street heaven was static. Those who ascended there were supposedly blissful, standing throughout eternity, arranged in rows according to rank. Hell, on the other hand, was busy—a subterranean factory, where torturers and victims all seemed to be working overtime in the flames. Earth was sandwiched between the two. The average person, seeing the grandeur of the heavenly hosts as shown in church paintings, could have little doubt as to where he was likely to end up. His future was made even clearer by the Mystery plays put on by his guild, where hell was shown as a monstrous yawning mouth with sharpened fangs, crowded with people much like himself. There was, of course, some hope: many could be purified in a place called purgatory and their sufferings there could be shortened by prayers, good deeds and other efforts made for them here on earth. Because saints and other holy beings had been so good, they had piled up a great store of extra merits which could be purchased by sinners. The less holy could save themselves and their dead loved ones by applying to the church for an "indulgence," or purchase of these merits. Wherever these indulgences were for sale, the money poured into the church. At a time when funds were thus being raised to build a new basilica of St. Peter's in Rome, Martin Luther objected, among other things, to this outflow of German money to the corrupt church in Italy. In 1517 he invited a debate by posting a list of ninety-five points for discussion on the church door in Wittenberg. The list included an attack on indulgences.

Luther's arguments were soon translated from Latin into German and widely spread, and it was not long before the Pope declared in a famous Bull: "Arise, O Lord . . . a wild boar has invaded Thy vineyard." And a brilliant Dutch scholar, Erasmus of Rotterdam, who tried to remain neutral, was writing: "This is no ordinary storm. Earth and air are convulsed." Erasmus correctly foresaw that the outcome would be frightful bloodshed.

Millions of people turned Protestant. Half of Germany became officially Protestant. England established its own national church in the days of Henry VIII, when the King dissolved the monasteries and took over their great wealth. Peasants, stirred up by Luther's words and their own hard lot, began to revolt in Central Europe, in an uprising called the Peasants' War. The Scandinavian countries eventually turned Protestant, while the struggles between Protestant Huguenots and the Catholics in France led to civil war. The Thirty Years' War between Europe's Catholics and Protestants which broke out in 1618 spread terrible ruin and cost Germany half her population.

Since Protestantism was based on each individual's interpretation of Scripture, and had no unifying center, it soon shattered into sects, with Lutheranism being but one of them. Nevertheless it promoted the love of goodness and truth, and the value of the average man. Many died as heroes for their beliefs. The "Puritans" were Protestants who wished to purify the Church of England. They were not so harsh and narrow as people now believe, but like all Protestants, they emphasized the Bible. America's Pilgrim Fathers, who wished to model life and law on Scripture, were Puritans who had separated from England's national church.

Other people rejected religion entirely. Still others remained Catholics but brought about reforms in the church. These three groups—Catholic, Protestant, and unbelieving—have continued on into our own times.

8 Art as a Way of Life

Had it not been for its explosion of great art, the Renaissance would surely not seem as splendid as it does. The very name of the age —Renaissance or rebirth—was coined by Vasari, an artist of the sixteenth century. Suddenly, large sums of money were being paid out to buy objects of beauty: furniture, clothes, jewelry, buildings, public and private, gardens, city squares. Wherever the eye gazed, it must behold a work of art. Art to enrich life became the order of the day. Men seemed to comprehend that even if they themselves were forgotten, their works of beauty would remain.

Of the many factors that produced this outburst, the most important were wealth and freedom. Artists began to experiment by the thirteenth century. Before this time, most painters and sculptors had earned their bread and cheese by decorating churches, which meant working on Biblical scenes and episodes from the lives of saints. The conservatism of the church had prevented them from experimenting; anything new was likely to be branded a heresy. But now the great families of Italy, newly powerful princes, wealthy merchants, city governments and foreign kings began to compete for the services of painters, jewelers, sculptors and architects. Women of wealth wanted themselves and their homes adorned. Their husbands hoped to win immortality through the brush of a great artist. Even the Popes were caught up in the new movement. In the sixteenth century Julius II tore down the ancient St. Peter's basilica, dating from the fourth century, to make way for something more significant. After being devoted so long to religious subjects, painting and sculpture adventured into the sunny fields and secret groves of nature. Instead of martyrs pierced with arrows, satyrs, nymphs, gods and goddesses from the old mythology emerged from banishment and began to be painted.

Church art did not disappear. Indeed, it became one of the glories of the Renaissance. The flat, formal "Byzantine" or Constantinople style of the fourteenth century gave way to a warmer, more human, three-dimensional portrayal of sacred figures. In the fifteenth century artists dissected bodies to learn their structure and used this knowledge in their work. Human figures took on natural grace and power, and in imitation, once again, of ancient Greeks were often depicted in the nude. The study of perspective brought depth to landscapes as well as a sharper reality to closed spaces. There were also new developments up north. The

An artist at work in his studio.

Inside the image, bottom center: *Ioan. Stradanus invent.   Phls Galle excud.*

Flemish painter Jan van Eyck was using a new oil medium which was quickly adopted by the Italians for easel painting. Oil paints not only added more subtle coloring and a finer sense of depth, but gave the painter a freedom to experiment and revise. This had never been possible with fresco painting, which was executed on walls, and not too easy with tempera, which was used on walls and wood. In fresco, which in Italian means fresh, the plaster was applied fresh, and only one day's quantity at a time. Then the artist went quickly to work, using paint in pure colors, mixed only with water. In the drying process, the paint became a part of the wall. Any changes made afterward looked patchy and did not last.

During the Middle Ages, painters and sculptors had been treated more as craftsmen than as artists. The Renaissance lifted some artists to a point where they were sought after by kings and consulted by Popes. But an artist belonged to a guild and still learned his trade much as if he were learning to dye cloth or tan leather. Generally this meant he undertook hard, intense work for little pay.

An artist's busy studio. At far right, older apprentices grind and mix colors.

Right:
An artist adds a few touches to his painting of a noblewoman's gown.

116

Apprentice Painter

How did a boy become an apprentice painter? Two or three memorable artists, notably Giotto and Mantegna, were shepherds, and were discovered when they showed exceptional skill in drawing sheep. In most cases, however, relatives or friends took samples of the boy's art to an established artist and tried to get him accepted as an apprentice—usually for a three-year term around the age of ten. "Welcome to my workshop," the master might say to a young hopeful. "Let your hands tell me what kind of a fellow you are." Giotto once answered this question by dipping a brush in red paint and drawing a perfect circle with one whirl of the wrist.

Except for the novelty and excitement of being in a workshop, an apprentice led a rather dreary life. He was given all the dirty work: cleaning brushes, smoothing down the wood panels that were often used instead of canvas, grinding pigments for paints, and learning to mix and apply plaster. He also worked on the "cartoons," which were actual-size drawings for a fresco or panel painting, with perforations along the lines of the picture. These cartoons were held against fresh plaster and the perforations were dusted, so that they left a dotted outline on the plaster as a guide to the painter. More often than not, the apprentice lived where he worked, and if he had the misfortune to be under contract to a miser, he slept under dirty covers and ate bad food.

Early in his training, an apprentice learned to mix and apply gesso: plaster of Paris and glue and water combined to a thin consistency and brushed onto a wood or canvas surface to prepare it for the artist. He ground colors and mixed them with water, white of egg or egg yolk or vinegar; sometimes he shredded a tender branch from a fig tree and mixed the sap into a beaten yolk. He had to know how, when and where each mixture was to be used. Even the great Leonardo da Vinci, eager to experiment, used the wrong medium for one of his masterpieces, *The Last Supper*. He painted it with oils on a plaster wall that was damp, and soon it began to flake.

In between his many chores, the boy apprentice received lessons in drawing and using the brush, not only from the master artist but from older apprentices. If he was lucky enough to be in a large workshop with many commissions, he might watch the specialists: men who lacked the ability to do a complete picture but were good at drawing hands, or painting embroidery to look as if some woman had stitched in the gold thread that very morning.

Finally, a great day came for the young apprentice. The master would point out a corner of some large work and tell him to paint

in a bit of background. Later, after years of training, when his brush had become swift and sure, the youth might be chosen as one of a team to paint a church fresco, a task where there was no place for mistakes and second tries.

Artists and Their Patrons

Once he was trained, a guild member, and authorized to set up his own shop, a young painter usually stayed on at his master's studio until he had won away some of the clientele. This was fair enough, since the master had enjoyed the youth's talent very cheaply over a period of several years. However, the young man's surest road to success was to acquire a wealthy patron. Rich men of today collect fine arts, but in the Renaissance they collected the artists themselves. Artists and writers were always on the lookout for a patron. Leonardo da Vinci, with six pupils, had the Duke of Milan for protector. When the Duke was driven out of his domains by the French, Leonardo worked in Venice and Mantua until a new patron, Cesare Borgia, took him on not as a painter but an architect and engineer. He was so versatile that he could also have served as sculptor, musician, anatomist, geographer, botanist, astronomer, chemist and mathematician. Cesare soon fell from power, but two kings of France became Leonardo's patrons later on.

A popular artist who had a patron enjoyed unusual freedom for the times, in the sense that he often had to be coddled and deferred to or he would not produce. "I said that I was born free, and free I mean to live," a young artist boasted. If attempts were made to

An author presents his work to a noble patron who has probably agreed to support him.

A sculptor's workshop, showing a bricklayer, stonemason, architect, and the sculptor himself completing a statue.

force him to work, his product would suffer, as a patron soon discovered. Like an egg, the artist was not to be stepped on.

Andrea Mantegna, typical of many artists, stayed fifty years at the court of Mantua. He was paid fifteen ducats a month (about sixty dollars), besides getting wheat, wood, wine and lodgings for himself and his family. Although often bad-tempered and given to complaining, he was tolerated as a valuable member of the household. Since artists might be loaned out by their patrons, the Pope borrowed Mantegna to paint a chapel, and the painter was away two years. Homesick, he wrote to say he was "a child of the house of Mantua" and wished to come back.

An artist could make his patrons wait. Isabella d'Este, who was accustomed to being instantly obeyed, had to wait many months before the jeweler Anichino would engrave a turquoise for her. When Leonardo promised but did not send a painting to her, a friend wrote: "I will not fail to entreat Leonardo, and also Perugino [to paint a picture]. . . . Both make liberal promises, and seem to have the greatest wish to serve Your Highness. Nevertheless, I think it will be a race between them which is the slower!"

Free as he was, an artist could still be jailed or banished by some tyrant of a patron. One patron wrote as follows to a Mantuan painter who had been told to decorate a little studio: "Since we have learned by experience that you are as slow in finishing your work as in everything else, we send this to remind you that if our *studiolo* is not finished on our return, we intend to put you in the dungeon of the castello. And this, we assure you, is no jest. . . ." One sculptor, dissatisfied with his pay, destroyed a statue of the Virgin that he had completed, and was jailed for it.

A Renaissance artist portrays a shy little girl's expression and clothing with a masterly realism.

Renaissance artists were individualists themselves and added to the cult of individuality through the beautiful portraits and busts they created. For this, tyrants paid them well, and powerful city-states like Florence and Venice, and kings like Francis I of France, eagerly sought them out.

Each artist had his quirks and could indulge them. One highly respected artist went about in such dirty, paint-stained clothes that, although he was born Tomasso Guido, he was called "Masaccio" or "Sloppy Tom." Another artist, who had herded cattle as a boy, made up for it later on by dressing in the finest clothes and setting a splendid table for his friends. His extravagances were such that he died as he had begun: poor.

Some artists became greedy for money. Pietro Perugino, who taught the immortal Raphael, was one of these. He earned a great deal and kept all his cash on him. He used to work with such intensity that when his wife called him to dinner he would cry: "Serve up the soup while I put another saint in." By contrast, there was the sculptor, Donatello, famed for reviving the Roman art of sculpture that stands free, instead of in relief or attached to a background. He cared so little about money that he tossed whatever he had into a basket that hung from the ceiling of his studio. Friends who were short of cash could reach up and take enough to tide them over.

A successful painter might make a business of art. He would simply lay out the design of a painting and then let his journeymen and apprentices work away at the less important parts. In contrast to this factory method another artist might be so jealous of his art that he trusted no one else to mix his paints.

However varied they might be, Renaissance artists were alike in their almost religious devotion to their work. While learning to paint, Perugino had no money for a bed, and slept on a chest. Ghirlandaio believed so strongly in his mission to make the world more beautiful that he had a standing rule to take any kind of artistic commission. He accepted even such ordinary tasks as decorating market baskets, and he himself would decorate them, if no one else would. Uccello, who greatly advanced the use of perspective, stayed in his room for months studying this subject. He often toiled long into the night and when reminded that he should get some sleep he would murmur: "This perspective! What a delight!" Another who worked nights as well as days was young Luca della Robbia. While it was light he labored with mallet and chisel; at night he drew, putting his feet in a basket of shavings to keep off the cold.

Giorgio Vasari, artist, businessman, courtier, who wrote of these men and their devotion, says: "It does not surprise me, since no man distinguishes himself in any art who is not ready to bear heat, cold, hunger and thirst. He who imagines that he can become great by taking his ease in pleasant surroundings is much mistaken." It was such sacrificial labor that produced the paintings and sculptures, the splendid buildings and monuments that have made the word Renaissance mean a great flourishing of the creative arts.

War and Violence

New weapons of war, such as cannon, which had already been introduced in the fourteenth century, were further developed and spread during the Renaissance. Italy provided the best place to see these new weapons and techniques at work. She was a prey to invaders from France, Germany, Hungary and Spain. She was also a battle-ground for her own warring city-states—the small, independent republics or principalities each built around a city such as Florence or Milan.

The frequent warfare among these city-states was once simple enough. Almost every spring, with the coming of good weather, the workers and merchants of one town or another would polish up their breast-plates, put their armor on and march out to settle a dispute with a rival city or to snatch a piece of someone else's land. Then—win, lose or draw—it was back to their shops and work benches.

War, however, was changing and the city-states faced a new problem: as armor-piercing arrows and then gunpowder came into use, a Renaissance warrior on horseback put on still heavier armor. This armor became so massive that by the sixteenth century cranes were sometimes brought along to lift the heaviest burdened knights into their saddles. Ludicrous as a man-at-arms appeared when dangling from the hook of a crane, a united charge by these human fortresses struck terror into the ranks of even the bravest men on foot.

Informal community armies could no longer cope with this kind of robot-like enemy. For example, on the field of Campaldino in 1289, the foot soldiers of Florence won only through the suicidal courage of individual soldiers. They plunged between murderous hooves and slashed the chargers' unprotected bellies with swords and daggers, thus bringing mount and rider down. Once he fell to the ground, it is true, a man-at-arms was helpless. Sometimes he suffocated in a smashed helmet. More frequently he was axed to death by foot soldiers as he lay like a beetle on its back. Nevertheless, the man-at-arms was a tower of strength, and usually he could not be defeated except by an enemy mounted and armed like himself.

Hired Soldiers and "Instant Cavalry"

The rulers of Italian city-states saw they would have to meet knight with knight. But they did not relish the high cost of turning their

Hammering out armor in a workshop of the early sixteenth century.

Overleaf:
Florence routs Siena at the Battle of San Romano in 1432. Broken lances litter the field.

part-time soldiers into full-time knights. A man-at-arms needed long training and had to be kept in practice, for a rusty knight was not much better than rusty armor. The new plate armor was expensive, and, in addition, two to three mounted men were needed to service each man-at-arms and his battle horse. This kind of war would not pay.

So the rulers found a cheaper answer: "instant" heavy cavalry. They hired men to fight for them. These men, already trained in so-called "Free Companies," had their own armor and organization. Except for their name, there was nothing free about them. On the contrary, they were out for all they could get. One of their leaders, the Count of Landau, stated their purpose clearly: "Our manner of life in Italy is universally known—to rob, to plunder, to kill those who resist." War had become big business. Knighthood still existed, but now it was often maintained only by robbing merchants— "figsacks" or "peppersacks," the German knights called them because of the merchandise they carried with them. Joining others like

A monster crossbow and projectiles used in sieges. This weapon could be swiveled around and cranked up and down.

themselves, the Free Companies made up armies of forty thousand or more and swept over the countryside like a deadly mowing machine.

Medieval armies had left a residue of ruffians in each invaded land—men who preferred fighting and looting to plowing a furrow. The men in the Free Companies, especially the foot soldiers, were described by a French writer as "scoundrels fit for hanging." They let their hair and beards grow wild and were apt to wear filthy, half-buttoned shirts that displayed their hairy chests. They also favored baggy pants ending at the knee, as well as torn stockings of different colors.

Cities like Florence and great families like the Visconti began to hire these mercenaries. The Pope, too, made use of them, one company being known by the bizarre title of "Brigands of the Pope." But such companies could not be trusted. They were a weapon that could also be bought by the enemy and turned against their former purchaser.

Because these outlaws could so easily be lured from one side to the other, their employers appointed overseers who went along to make sure the companies fulfilled the terms of their contract. Their loyalty was so uncertain that employers often kept the leaders' wives and children as hostages. The companies also had a sound method for discouraging too much zeal in their mercenary opponents: if the latter fought too hard and delayed the outcome, once the battle was over the victor would hang some of them.

Along with the mercenary soldiers came judges to arbitrate disputes, notaries to draw up contracts, priests to see to the welfare of souls, money-lenders, and hosts of disreputable camp followers, both men and women. Some of these came willingly, others at dagger point. The treasurer paid salaries and divided the booty. The companies held huge markets to turn the spoils of war into cash. Nor did the Italian banks hesitate to accept these outlaws' loot as legal tender and to pay interest on deposits of this kind.

The Ruthless Captains

At the top of each of these "wandering military states" stood the *condottiere*, the captain or leader. His decisions in battle were not to be questioned and he could be arbitrary on other occasions as well.

Large additions to the incomes of the leaders accumulated from the sale of what we would call "protection." The *condottieri* black-mailed popes, cities, and great families with threats to make war on them or lay waste their lands. They held rich men for ransom and tortured the victims if the money was slow in arriving. Worst of all were their attacks on the innocent. They carried off cattle, set fire to harvests, ruined vines and orchards, burned homes, raped and slaughtered, and even murdered babies.

They were equally ruthless with their own kind. When one of the early captains, called the "Archpriest," grew too old for war, his company solved the problem by killing him. One city council, debating how best to reward a certain captain-general who had served them well, reached this conclusion: "Let us put him to death. Then we can worship him as our patron saint."

Italian soldiers of ability soon recognized the opportunity offered by the Free Companies for climbing to the top. Since success and plenty of booty came only through brilliant leadership, the mercenaries

German wheellock pistols of the late sixteenth century. Such guns were expensive and were engraved like works of art.

would follow any man who could win, no matter what his birth. Sometimes the leader was a noble. The Duke of Urbino was said never to have lost a battle. He was one captain whose word could be trusted. He used the people from his own lands as soldiers, and enriched his own territories with the spoils won abroad. He was so popular at home that people would kneel in the street as he passed and say: "God keep you."

Another leader, Francesco Sforza, who became Duke of Milan, rose from peasant stock. His father was also a captain-general, whose house was "an arsenal and a fortress." The son became so famous that the mere sight of him on the battlefield would make men lay down their weapons. His enemies would doff their helmets and welcome him as "the father of all us men-at-arms." Reputations like his could only be won through a true capacity for leading men. There is even an instance where one leader, known as Boldrino, commanded his troops after he was dead. Boldrino had died but until his men could decide on who should replace him, his body was embalmed and his flag kept flying above his closed tent. From time

A "peace campaign." Under the legend, "Peace enriches the citizens," prosperous inhabitants are collecting funds. At right, under the legend, "War enriches the foreigners," the money is being paid to foreign mercenaries.

to time a courier would hurry out of the tent, bringing commands as if from Boldrino.

When turmoil was expected in a city, because of a change of government or the approach of an enemy, the leading citizens would hire bands of soldiers to defend their palaces. They might ask a likely young man to recruit fifty companions for this purpose, and would pay and lodge them well. At such times, however, country people might flock into a city for protection and find no guards to defend them. When Rouen was besieged in the early fifteenth century, twelve thousand of these refugee peasants were forced back out of the city gates and they starved between the besieging army and the walls.

As is usual in warfare, a better offense gradually led to an improved defense: the heavily armored rider was confronted with the phalanx,

A crossbowman holds the bolt in his mouth while bending his bow with a crannequin, a kind of jack.

Protective helmets were fancifully shaped and adorned.

a massed formation of foot-soldiers like that used by the ancient Greeks. With the phalanx came the pike, a long spear, its shaft, which was sometimes eighteen feet long, tipped with steel. Defending forces would plant the blunt end of their pikes firmly against the ground and point the weapons toward the onrushing cavalry. Since the men stood shoulder to shoulder, row on row, the charging knights had either to rein in or else impale themselves and their horses on this hedge of thorned steel.

The Revolution of the Cannon

Nevertheless, the phalanx and the long pike were soon swept from the field of battle. Ironically, the same weapon that doomed them destroyed their foe, the heavily armored knight. A cannonball could make powder alike of armor, phalanx and steel-tipped spear. In the beginning, the cannon frightened more men than it killed. Its thunderous blast panicked both rider and horse, but the stone cannon-balls did not always land on target. For one thing, the guns would blow up. Gunpowder varied greatly in explosive power and the cannon was often made of poorly wrought iron or had flaws in the casting. Men willing to risk their lives operating these infernal machines were thought to be working for the Devil, and the smell of brimstone that hung about them probably strengthened this belief.

An ornate Italian helmet of the mid-sixteenth century. The hole suggests that its wearer may not have survived the battle.

As the cannon foundries made their product more accurate and less dangerous to those who used them, there began a race to turn out ever larger guns. These giant cannons were given women's names, such as "Mad Margaret," which is still on display at Ghent. Mad Margaret weighs nearly seventeen tons. She fired a stone cannon-ball eight feet in circumference and weighing six hundred pounds. Obviously, such enormous guns were difficult to maneuver, and were mostly reserved for sieges where they could batter down thitherto invulnerable walls. Smaller cannon were employed in the field. The first to put cannon on wheels may have been the Venetians, who used oxen to draw them. The French substituted horses and devised a wagon frame from which the rear wheels could be quickly detached. On the march, their guns moved almost as quickly as the infantry—a great marvel then.

The French army of the late fifteenth century was a model for Europe. Besides improvements in the art of war, the French developed an excellently drilled, maneuverable infantry, well equipped with pikes and halberds (a combination spear, hook and battle-axe).

Attackers aiming siege guns at a town wall. The aiming mechanism is shown at left.

Much of modern weaponry goes surprisingly far back in time. For example, today's machine guns have an ancestor called a *ribaldequin:* it was discovered that small guns joined to each other in a horizontal line could be fired in a series when a single man touched off the fuse powder of each gun in quick succession. But these early machine guns had a serious defect: after the first sweeping volley had been fired, the separate reloading of each barrel used up precious time. If the ribaldequin failed to stop the enemy with its first blast it might be captured before it could be fired again.

The ultimate in this type of weapon appeared in 1387. It stood twenty feet high and consisted of one hundred and forty-four gun barrels massed in a three-story structure. Antonio della Scala, Lord of Verona, dispatched three of these contrivances to annihilate the Paduan army, but soft ground lay between them and the battlefield.

Despite all that horses could do, these instruments of destruction bogged down and never fired a shot.

A military camp site.

From Matchlock to Musket

This failure seems to have dulled enthusiasm for such grandiose devices. Inventors increasingly gave their attention to improving the most mobile weapon of all: the individual gun for the individual soldier. No fixed date can be assigned for the first use of small firearms—just as there is uncertainty as to the earliest use of cannon. Oddly enough, the latter appear to have been used first. There is good reason to believe the Germans had cannon when they fought

Overleaf:
A naval battle in 1499.
Arrows, rocks and cannon-
balls were rained on Turks
who tried to board Venetian
ships.

the Italians at Cividale in 1331, but not for another quarter of a century do we find a mention of small firearms. A primitive musket was actually a small cannon, consisting of a short iron tube attached to the end of a stick from three to four feet long. The tube was solid at the back end and the charge of gunpowder was rammed in through the open end of the weapon, as in a cannon. When a flame was applied to the touchhole, the gun would fire.

Before it could become a serious threat to the enemy this "hand cannon" had to undergo a number of changes. The stick on which it was mounted eventually became today's stock, and a fire pan was added just below the touchhole. Priming powder sprinkled onto the pan could easily be ignited, exploding the charge inside.

The next step was the invention of a "match" made of a long fibre soaked in saltpetre. Then someone came up with a revolutionary device called a matchlock, which would hold a burning match ready at all times to strike the pan of priming powder. Now the soldier could keep his eyes on the target because he no longer needed to direct the lighted match; and he had the full use of both hands. But the matchlock had its weaknesses, for unless the burning match was set aside while the user loaded his gun, he might blow himself up. Also, the glowing end warned the enemy of a night attack, and it was soon quenched by rain. Matchlocks were the choice of armies all through the Renaissance. The weapon gradually acquired a longer and heavier barrel, which had to be rested on a forked prop stuck into the ground. During the two centuries that lay between the "hand cannon" and the "musket," as this heavier gun was now called, a great advance in both power and accuracy had taken place. When the Spanish army used it under the Duke of Alva in the sixteenth century, the musket was so powerful it could bring down a horse at a distance of five hundred yards.

Soldiers attacking a private home.

Torture, Thugs and Sudden Death

It was a time of sudden turns of fortune, of riches to rags in an hour. The mother of a disgraced official in Rome was driven out of her mansion and, left with only the clothes she had on, hurried from friend to friend seeking help. Afraid of being punished, they turned her away and closed their doors. Worse than hardness of heart was brutality. The history of Europe in the Renaissance is stained with torture scenes that are unbearable to read; torture was legally used by the authorities and all kinds of violence were common.

The lack of a well-organized police force, the contempt for man as a hopeless sinner, the small value of life when so many died young from diseases and wars, the unimportance of the ordinary man when unrepresented in government and exploited by his "betters"—these are some of the reasons that torture was an everyday matter. Our own century has perfected mass killing, but most modern men seem to be more sensitive than Renaissance men when it comes to inflicting physical pain. We havce soieties to protect animals from cruelty and most civilians are no longer allowed to witness executions. We are not used to the sight of people hanging from a gallows, the bodies, as the French poet François Villon in the mid-fifteenth century described them in his "Ballad of the Hanged," swaying in the wind. We have the electric chair but not the Iron Maiden of Nuremberg, which grasped the victim with its iron arms and pressed him against iron spikes.

There was also much quarreling and fighting in private life. Women carried on feuds, soldiers kidnapped young girls, thieves went about in bands, men beat their wives, housewives struck their maids, and neighbors hurled oaths as well as insults at one another on the street. Practically every man and woman went armed with a knife, or was escorted by others so armed. Duelling was frequent because it was a recognized way of proving one's manliness. Well into the sixteenth century, the city-state of Ferrara permitted a duel to continue until one of the participants was killed. Even boys were permitted to duel: they fought each other with knives. Less bloody but not less deadly were those "games of stones" which the youth of Florence played at carnival time. These began with singing and dancing around huge bonfires in the squares and ended with rock-throwing battles that left a few dead bodies on the paving stones.

Laws were passed to stop such games, but had as little effect as other laws against violence. Florentines who complained to the police of criminal assaults were in danger of being stabbed to death the next time they ventured out at night. And judges brave enough to sentence wrongdoers went in fear of their lives. The situation in Rome was no better. Indeed, the Rome of that day lay partially in ruins, and the inhabitants, who spoke many different dialects, were described as less Roman than barbarian. Pilgrims were preyed on and often murdered for the gold hidden in their clothes. A merchant who happened to be in a boat on the Tiber River, which passes through the heart of Rome, saw a corpse being heaved into the cloudy waters. When he was later asked why he had not reported this crime to the governor, he replied that on a hundred occasions he had seen bodies thrown in at that spot, a refuse dump, and no one had ever shown any interest in these crimes before. A prisoner who managed to escape from Rome's Castle St. Angelo broke his leg going over the wall; when he at last crawled through the city gate, he was attacked by a pack of wild dogs. Even so he felt himself lucky not to have died in the castle's dungeon, where captives were often thrown into a pit deep underground and starved to death.

Important people kept their own thugs and used them to put their enemies out of the way. When unable to make use of these "bravoes" they would try poison. Lest they themselves be poisoned, a few kings and nobles hired tasters who sampled each dish and goblet as it was served. France's King Charles VIII had his wine certified for him by a man who used a magical gold chain with a piece of horn attached to it; horn was thought to be an antidote to poison. Others might try out their food and drink on pets, or even guests. Slow-acting poisons, which kept the victim from dying immediately after dinner, were much in demand, for if he died a few weeks later, it was hard to trace the murderer. Poisonings were so common that few leaders went to their graves without a suspicion of foul play. A family would retaliate, avenging a member's death, whereupon a vendetta or feud for blood revenge would be under way.

Official violence, torture and murder continued as in the Middle Ages. No one worried about a criminal's rights, and terrible tortures were used to make an accused man confess. His legs might be encased in wet leather boots that caused intense pain as they shrank over a low fire. The Bretons sometimes fastened a man in an iron chair that they pushed nearer and nearer to a flaming furnace. The Italians suspended a man horizontally with ropes tied to his ankles and wrists, the only support being a pointed stake at the base of his spine. To make sure he did not die before he had gasped out a confession, they kept taking him down, reviving him with stimulants and then putting him to the torture again. Even those who were condemned to death were sometimes tortured, either as part of their sentence, or to make them name their accomplices.

A few victims, however, usually noblemen or gentlemen, were beheaded rather than hanged because the chopping block was thought to be kinder and less humiliating than the gallows. A device similar to the guillotine was used as early as the thirteenth century in Italy for removing the heads of nobles, and other instruments of this sort are depicted in German engravings of the sixteenth century. Nevertheless, the two-handed sword and the headsman's axe were still the most widely employed means for dispatching the nobly born. Efficient German executioners were held in some esteem; certain ones even gained a rank in the nobility. In France, however, executioners were obliged at times to wear a distinctive red or yellow coat. They were forbidden to live within the city limits, except in the area where criminals were pilloried; for the "King's Sworn Tormentor," as the executioner was called, was thought to be

Bravoes about to kill a helpless victim in the street.

A man being "drawn and quartered" by four horses. Executioners urge the horses on.

ill-omened. Nevertheless, he received high pay and other rewards. Many believed he had healing powers and that he was better than any doctor in setting dislocated limbs. A cure-all which he sold was much in demand: the fat of a hanged criminal.

To sum up this violence, we could say that Christian meekness was not much in evidence during the Renaissance. Instead, men preferred to display a pagan "manliness." In Italy, especially, the thing to do was to show a greater bravery than the other man, or more strength, or quickness with a knife. And if one died on the gallows for one's deeds, the thing to do was to die bravely like an ancient Roman.

Warfare in the Renaissance, however, moved on toward modern times. In the sixteenth century troops were outfitted with uniforms. The first bomb was exploded in 1588. Telescopes were used not long afterward to spy out the movements of the enemy. The first "war game" was played early in the seventeenth century, when William Louis of Friesland planned his battles by deploying toy soldiers on a large map. In these and other ways already discussed, war was adapting to the requirements of a new age.

10 Travel by Land and by Sea

Going on journeys was much in the spirit of the Renaissance. The rebirth of interest in this world, the break-up of the medieval manor units which held so many people bound to the soil, and the far horizons which now beckoned, drew many from their homes. Even though the hardships of travel were still very great, Renaissance people traveled much more than is generally supposed. Not only did soldiers, sailors, merchants, diplomats and scholars go a-wandering; but so did royal brides—numerous in a day of many small states; specialists such as master craftsmen, with their apprentices; kings and queens on affairs of great moment; clergymen journeying for the church, and monks or nuns on convent business. There were also thousands of ordinary people going to see friends, or to visit a health resort, or quite simply off on a junket. Although crusades were a thing of the past, many a traveler was also making a pilgrimage.

The shrines that were popular might be far away from the pilgrim's home. They included such places as Canterbury and Westminster in England; St. James of Compostela in Spain; Ephesus in Asia Minor, traditional home of Mary; Rome; and even Jerusalem. Often, the reason for the pilgrimage was a vow that had been made at a critical time, perhaps when someone had a life-and-death illness. If the person making the vow was unable to go himself, he might well send another in his stead.

People traveled in groups for greater safety, and they took supplies along with them, since it might be difficult to get food and other necessaries on the way, many peasants tending to hide their stores. When royalty traveled, the equivalent of a whole town with its provisions might accompany them. The alternative was to prey on the peasants.

Queen Elizabeth of England doted on making royal journeys from palace to palace, taking along all kinds of supplies, perhaps even down to the window glass. Sometimes she could not make up her mind whether to stay longer in a place or move on, and hundreds or even thousands of people remained in suspense. Once when the court was half packed and the carter had been summoned for the third time only to be dismissed, he said disgustedly: "Now I see that the Queen is a woman just like my wife." Elizabeth, standing at the window, overheard him, laughed, and sent him some coins. When the King of France traveled he would be accompanied by at least twelve thousand people—so the goldsmith Cellini reports.

A traveler returns from a sea voyage. Although depicting the story of Ulysses, the painter has used Renaissance figures and settings.

This meant of course that every lodging along the way was taken over, and weary travelers who were following the court said afterward: "We set up canvas tents like gypsies."

From Mules to Gilded Cages

Besides horses and mules, donkeys and oxen were the main transport animals. There were all kinds of horses: pureblooded Turkish mounts, given as presents to kings; race horses bred for speed alone; chargers for war, all weight and muscle, strong enough to carry a man in armor; draft horses; palfreys for ladies to ride and for church processions—all the way down to sorry nags. Like a car today, a man's horse was a status symbol. Travelers would exchange hired mounts for fresh ones at relay stations. Other travelers could then hire a horse going back to its home stable. Rented horses, however, were not always of the best, and they often went lame, being carelessly shod.

Delicately bred ladies and the sick would travel in cushion-strewn litters which were mounted on shafts and borne by mules or horses, one animal at each end. Also in use were clumsy carts, some having a cloth canopy. In 1509, a large, comfortable type of coach was brought into Italy from Hungary. During the same period, the wide streets of Milan were thronged with beautiful carriages, carved and gilded, some drawn by four horses, and many by two. Florence began to have four-wheeled vehicles by 1534.

Perils of the Road

The people of that day were not so clock-conscious and time-ridden as we are. The majority did not have watches, but relied on church bells, dawn trumpets, noon guns and the like; they were likely to make an appointment for such a time as "an hour after sunset." A short period was described as "time enough to say two Ave Marias." Travel time varied because of the hazards and the fact that people stopped to rest and visit friends en route. In 1428 a lady left Genoa September 6th and reached her destination—Milan—October 8th, having covered a distance of only one hundred and twenty miles. The normal ride from Perugia to Urbino, sixty-four miles, took two days. But special couriers were rapid; a letter could go from Paris to Avignon in southern France in about four days, and to Avignon from Rome in about ten.

Roads were often only tracks. Traces of old Roman roads still remain today, but the fine, dressed stone with which they were paved might be dug up by some individual to put into a house he was building. Another hazard was random dumping onto the highway: a galloping horse could not always see, in time, a heap of plaster and broken tiles barring the way. Again, the traveler might come to a lake several miles wide, where he and his companions would have the choice of giving up their journey or taking to the water, with their horses, in a light pine boat. If the traveler made the other side, he might, although clothed in mail, wearing heavy

boots and carrying a gun, have to urge his horse up an almost vertical mountain path.

People crossing the Alps had to be of heroic mold. When going through the St. Gotthard Pass during warmer weather, they would fire off guns to bring down a threatening avalanche before crossing through. The traveler sat on an ox-drawn sled, followed by his horse led by the reins. The ox, going ahead on a long rope, would thus generally be the only victim in case of an accident. Elsewhere the Alpine traveler rode through the mist of thundering waterfalls, and over bridges which in some places were nothing but giant fir trees laid across a chasm. Making his way along a dizzy ledge, he would close his eyes and leave all to the sure-footed mules. It was also hardly reassuring to a traveler to know that the area was infested

Pilgrims seeking a place to spend the night. Medals on their hats proclaim the shrines they have visited.

with bears and wolves. Nor did he have much to look forward to, for the day's danger and toil would end, if he was lucky, in a mountaineer's house half buried in snow. Here, after a little cheese, milk, and bad wine, the stranger would climb up into a cupboard, and shiver all night between a thin mattress and cover stuffed with feathers. From October until the following spring, such a journey over the Alps could not be made at all.

When taking a long sea journey the traveler would have to provide for himself much as an explorer might today. He would bring along live poultry and sheep, spirits, biscuits, a supply of drugs in case of sickness, and even a quantity of snow to cool his drinks. Some countries already required passports—that is, papers allowing the traveler to leave. In some areas he had to produce a bill of health. England would not let him export money, even foreign money, and could detain his luggage. There were many customs posts and toll houses along the rivers. On the Loire between Roanne and Nantes, a distance of less than four hundred miles, tolls had to be paid almost seventy-five times, say an average of one stop every five miles, and it was not very different by land.

Robbery and murder, in that day of war and violence, were not unusual hazards of travel. Highwaymen haunted the road between London and Cambridge. In France, there were tribes of brigands, and although numbers of them were hanged, others took their place. As sunset came on, travelers would hasten to reach the shelter of a walled town, because the gates would be closed at dusk. This gradually led to the custom of building inns outside the walls. One might imagine that walls around a city gave the inhabitants a sense of security; unfortunately, many who were walled in ought to have been walled out.

Innkeepers Good and Bad

It must not be assumed that the travelers were always innocent victims. A party might rent a boat, and another party might then come up and try to get the vessel away by force. One surly innkeeper, who had insisted on being paid the night before, reckoned without his guest: on leaving, the guest took out his knife and slit the four beds to ribbons. Usually, the innkeeper had the traveler at his mercy, and travelers' complaints included everything from a mattress stuffed with leaves, which pricked the guest and crackled all night, to bad food and vermin. One man expressed the general attitude when he was summoned to Italy from Switzerland in 1523. Explaining

Hungry wayfarers are fed at a monastery.

why he would not go there, he wrote: "The road over the Alps is long. The lodgings on the way are dirty and inconvenient. The smell of the stoves is intolerable. The wine is sour and disagrees with me." To improve the situation, gentlemen might band together and establish an inn under a carefully chosen host. A rich old man might arrange to live in such an inn for the rest of his life. In some accounts, indeed, we find nothing but praise for inns and taverns, especially those on well-traveled routes, and some monasteries also provided a haven along the way.

Arriving at a well-run inn, the traveler would be greeted by the sight of a great wooden and iron wheel revolving over a good fire. On the spokes and rim of the wheel were chickens, pheasants and partridges, thrushes, larks, wild ducks and pigeons. The thrushes would come to the table stuffed with sage and bread. If an oven-baked goose was preferred, it was filled with garlic and quince. Available dishes might include fish caught in the marshes and fried in oil with rosemary leaves, or a popular river-fish served in vinegar. After making his choice, and having, perhaps, a dish of salami and figs, the customer could order a dessert of pan-fried millet and chestnut pudding. Crisp macaroons were also a specialty.

When some notable event brought crowds to the city, a landlord might have to put guests in every alcove or even refuse more clients. The story has come down about a harassed innkeeper who put each new arrival in a bed and, as soon as he fell asleep, transferred him to the floor to make room for the next one.

A typical European journey by land and water, say from Basel, Switzerland via the river to Mainz, and then to Aachen, Germany, could involve many stages and changes. The journey down the Rhine should have been easy enough, but the boats carried no provisions and would put ashore at various places where the passengers, as captive customers, were often cheated. Here they could expect abominable food, overpowering smells, swarms of flies and a long wait. At night they did not sleep on board, but were sent to taverns where as many as sixty people would be crammed into a small, noisy and dirty central room. A supper of sorts would appear, and as the wine circulated, the noise increased, and many could neither eat nor sleep. A lucky traveler might have friends to visit overnight. But if he arrived in the midst of a bad storm, his host's larder might be bare. If illness struck a person while traveling, a closed carriage, drawn by four horses, might be hired, but the jolting over flint-hard, bumpy roads was most painful. Or the patient might be wrapped up and carried in a chair or even in a kind of basket. Sometimes he survived.

The First Gypsies

One fascinating kind of traveler remains to be mentioned. A chronicler tells of a hundred people arriving in Bologna, Italy, on the eighteenth of July, 1422, and camping within and outside the city gate. Their leader was a certain "André, Duke of Egypt." The townspeople went out to see them, and especially to see the Duke's wife, because it was rumored that she could foretell future events. The "Egyptian" women—known today as gypsies—walked about Bologna in groups, telling fortunes and pushing into shops, and the inhabitants soon found that many of their possessions had mysteriously disappeared. The gypsies said they had been banished by the Sultan of Turkey and were on a pilgrimage to Rome. In the beginning they received passports and letters promising them safe passage, but laws were soon enacted throughout Europe against these strange, wandering bands.

They were a dark-skinned people, the men with curly hair and the women with coarse, black pony-tails. They read palms and were full of tricks, such as paying townspeople with good money in the beginning, and passing counterfeit coins when about to leave. If, however, they settled for a time in a village, they usually did their

A scholar interested in navigation works out a problem in his study.

serious stealing elsewhere. They had a way with horses, and some worked in iron, and others were entertainers, turning double somersaults or dancing on a tightrope. Welcome or not, they hid here and there all over Europe, lived in a world within a world, and traveled light.

The Great Discoverers

For a thousand years, there had been little exploration of the earth by Christian peoples. Withdrawn into themselves, they were told to forget the world and turn their attention to heaven.

But the Renaissance changed all that. Men turned their eyes back to earth and explored it with eager curiosity. To learn more about the earth, one of the first areas they had to conquer was the open sea. So great explorations became a feature of the period. But the average man had a terror of the deep. The ocean was as mysterious as space is now. It was, many said, peopled with strange beings—described in travelers' accounts and the rediscovered classics. Lines from Shakespeare's play *The Tempest* expressed this fear:

> Full fathom five thy father lies;
> Of his bones are coral made;
> Those are pearls that were his eyes . . .
> Sea-nymphs hourly ring his knell . . .
> Now I hear them,—ding-dong, bell.

On the Mediterranean Sea, people traveled in galleys, hugging the shore and putting into port overnight. With good reason, many dreaded that journey. Cardinals having to return from Avignoñ to Rome well knew they might be blown off course and shipwrecked. They might have to watch as a galley laden with all their worldly goods and treasures was sucked down before their eyes; and they might, if lucky, be washed up on some empty, stony island.

In medieval times, the Saracens to the east were an obstacle to Europe's trade in that direction. And with the conquest of Constantinople in 1453 by the Turks, Portugal and Spain began to look both east and west in their search for new trade routes. Great riches were involved. It is not surprising that returned sailors did nothing to calm men's fears of the deep. Wishing to protect their trade secrets, they brought back stories of monsters and boiling seas.

Portugal's prince, called Henry the Navigator although he did not do much sailing, set himself the task of aiding and encouraging explorers. He established a sea-exploration center on Cape St. Vincent, the southwestern tip of continental Europe. Prince Henry studied all the maps and charts provided by his learned Arab, Jewish and other assistants, and hung on the words of shipmasters returned from long journeys. He was also scientific and practical, building a naval base where ships could be outfitted for exploration. Most Portuguese expeditions during the fifteenth century headed southward along the African coast. Bartholomew Diaz discovered the Cape of Good Hope in 1488. Nine years later (that is, five years after Columbus had reached the New World), Portugal's Vasco da Gama made the first voyage to India by way of the Cape.

Columbus was by no means the first man to believe the world was round. Some of the ancients had had this idea, long before. As far back as the sixth century B.C., the Greek philosopher Pythagoras had pondered the fact that ships sailing away into the distance gradually drop from sight, and from this he deduced that the earth was a sphere.

Genoa-born, from his boyhood Columbus had loved the sea; he became a mariner and went, he said, "wherever ship had sailed."

Defenseless travelers being murdered by mercenary soldiers in the countryside.

But in typical Renaissance fashion he became a scholar, too, studied maps and old writings and the technicalities of navigation as then known. He was urged onward by his conviction of a spiritual goal as well as the desire for riches. He wanted to take the Christian faith to the ends of the earth.

Like other geniuses of the Renaissance, Columbus looked for a patron. When Italy and Portugal, England and France turned him down, he came at last to Ferdinand and Isabella, the rulers of Spain. The Queen replied that if she had to, she would even pawn her jewels to help. What Columbus offered was far more than jewels: it was his life.

Caravels and Their Crews

Explorers of that day rarely got their choice of ships, for governments were unwilling to invest much money in vessels that might never

come back. Consequently, the vessel used by explorers was likely to be of the caravel type, sound and maneuverable enough but small. While the largest ship of the fifteenth century, the carrack, might carry a thousand toneladas of wine, a caravel could take aboard only sixty or seventy. (A tonelada which was used to measure a ship's capacity, was a large wine cask taking up about forty cubic feet of space.) Besides being small, a caravel had a clumsy shape. It has been compared to half a barrel sawed lengthwise and fitted with a superstructure at each end. Unfortunately no one knows the exact dimensions of Columbus' caravels the *Pinta* and the *Niña*, but few caravels exceeded eighty feet and his were probably much shorter. Such a vessel, small and relatively top-heavy, seemed to sail along on the surface of the water rather than in it. During heavy weather

The Portuguese land in far-off Brazil. They first went there in 1500.

the ship did not plow through the waves but rode up a wave and down the other side, making a passenger seasick even to think about it. Nevertheless, the caravel was a stout ship.

Larger vessels would carry craftsmen as part of the crew. The carpenter, probably the most necessary, had to repair hull, masts or anything made of wood. If shipwrecked, he alone might, by fashioning some sort of boat, save a crew from starving on some barren shore. A caulker was responsible for keeping the ship watertight. Before the voyage he had to coat the hull with tallow, perhaps mixed with pitch, for it was believed that this would keep off sea worms. The ship was not put into drydock, but floated onto a beach at high tide and heaved over as the tide ebbed. Seams were also coated with hot pitch. Once aboard, the caulker was kept hard at work, for all wooden ships leaked. The cooper, skilled in making and repairing

In vessels like this, or even smaller, the great explorers braved unknown seas.

wooden casks, supervised the vital containers of water, wine and vinegar. Partly because the water turned bad on a long voyage, but mostly from custom, sailors drank much wine, each man downing about a quart and a half per day. Some fresh water was also caught during rain storms.

All responsibility for food supplies fell on the steward. Ships stores ran mostly to dried and salted food: dried peas, lentils and beans; cheese, salt fish, casks of pork and beef pickled in brine. For bread there was hard ship's-biscuit baked ashore and kept in a dry place; or bannock, a flat loaf baked in hot ashes, quite salty, since the flour was salted to discourage weevils. (The English admiral Sir John Hawkins, who believed in smaller crews and better food, was the first to carry a supply of oranges for his men.)

Cooking was a problem. Stoves had only recently come into use on dry land, and there were none at sea. Instead, a wide, shallow iron box or tray was partially filled with sand, and an open wood fire built on this. Stews and fried food were thus favored, although some baking and roasting could be done by burying covered iron pots in banked coals. Hot meals were not practical just when they were needed most: in stormy weather. So great was the fire hazard in a wooden ship that the boatswain himself had to check the extinguished cookfire every night.

Master and pilot were the two top officers of a caravel. Masters were not yet the absolute dictators they became later on; at this period they had to win the men's confidence and good will. Next in the chain of command, but as well paid, was the pilot. Before ships ventured away from coastal waters, his job had been to guide his ship past dangerous currents, shoals and rocks; now he had to journey where his pilotage counted for nothing. In especially valuable ships, both master and pilot might be under a captain—not a seaman at all, but a merchant concerned with profit rather than navigation.

The captain or master had his own cabin in the high stern of the ship, well away from the stench of the hold. He had cabin boys to bring him his relatively better meals. The crew sought shelter wherever they might. In good weather they preferred to sleep on deck, usually on the hatch, which was flat. Often, the men had to sleep below on the cargo or ballast. The hold developed a horrible odor as the days wore on; pumps never could empty out all the bilge water, which smelled of dead rats and filth. Not much was done to keep either the ship or the crew clean. There was nothing but cold salt water for either bathing or laundry, and no tubs, so that sailors turned the job over to nature for long periods, and waited for rain. Beards were allowed to grow; feet were bare and unwashed;

and clothes were often in tatters since each man furnished his own.

Of all the able seamen, the one who steered the ship had the greatest responsibility. Using a tiller, a long horizontal shaft that passed through a hole in the stern, this man worked the huge rudder hinged to the stern. When the helmsman, guided by his compass, wanted the ship to go to starboard, he moved the tiller to port, and vice versa. There were large vessels that required as many as a dozen men to control the tiller in a storm. A second compass was placed on the quarter-deck and the pilot kept an eye on this, shouting orders into the steerage through an opening in the deck, for the man at the tiller could not see where the ship was going. (Although portable timepieces came in at the end of the fifteenth century, the watches or intervals on shipboard were timed with a half-hour sand glass.) To know how deep the water was, the pilot listened to the cries of the man who heaved the lead. Leads were of two kinds: a heavy one, around fourteen pounds, for deep sea soundings; and one half as heavy for use in shallow waters. Because it took a long time for a heavy or "dipsey" lead to reach bottom, the ship was halted during the process, but in shoal waters the vessel continued under way while the leadsman cast his lead and sang out the varying depths.

This is the type of voyaging Columbus knew on his mission. Although he was received back with joy, at least from his first venture, and Ferdinand and Isabella actually rose up from their thrones to greet him, it must not be supposed that all Europe at once grasped the implications of his discovery. Christian tradition still said the earth was flat. Europeans were, however, ready to accept every rumor of what he had found. Typical of Europe's first reaction was a letter by two servants, sent from Mantua to Spain to buy horses for their Duke. They wrote from Cadiz about "a Savona sailor named Columbus," and how he had come back with gold, pepper, sandalwood, red parrots as big as falcons, and twelve Indians. He had, they added, found wool-bearing trees. Ponzone, a scholar then at Ferrara, wrote: "I hear that a man named Columbus lately discovered an island . . . men of our height but of copper-colored skin . . . the women have faces as big as wheels . . . , they seem intelligent and are very tame and gentle."

Isabella died, leaving Columbus without hope. After his four voyages, he was poor and exhausted. The great admiral himself died at Valladolid, Spain, in his middle fifties. He died thinking he had been to Eastern Asia, even though he had never delivered the letter he had first taken with him, written by King Ferdinand to the Grand Khan of Tartary.

Epilogue

The Renaissance can be described in several ways: it was the highest stage of medieval life. It was a revival of pre-Christian Greece and Rome. It was the beginning of the modern world. Perhaps it could best be summarized thus:

Chance gave a handful of men wealth and absolute power and a few decades of time. These men became patrons of others who were geniuses in many fields: classical studies, religion, science, exploration, and especially art. The artists named the Renaissance and immortalized its visible splendor. Like its own well-loved fireworks, the Renaissance finally burst in blinding glory and passed by. But it was a period in time that people will always look back to, and remember.

Index

Picture Credits

P. 7 Rijksmuseum, Amsterdam; p. 8 (left) Pierpont Morgan Library, (right) The Metropolitan Museum of Art, N.Y., Bequest of Helen Hay Whitney, 1945; p. 9 Frick Art Reference Library; pp. 10–11 The Cleveland Museum of Art, The Holden Collection; p. 12 (top) Staatsbibliothek, Berlin, (bottom) Bibliothèque Nationale, Paris; p. 13 Bibliotheque Royale de Belgique; pp. 14–15 Soprintendenze alle Gallerie, Florence (Scala); pp. 16–17 Worchester Art Museum; p. 19 Galleria dell'Accademia, Venice (Alinari); p. 20 NYPL; p. 21 The Metropolitan Museum of Art, N.Y., Whittelsey Fund, 1949; p. 22 Yale University Library, Rare Books (Loebel); p. 23 Bargello, Florence (Scala); p. 24 NYPL; pp. 26 and 27 both Yale University Library, Rare Books (Loebel); p. 29 Galleria dell'Accademia, Venice (Bildarchiv Foto Marburg); p. 30 S. Anastasia, Verona (Scala); p. 33 The Metropolitan Museum of Art, N.Y., The Jules S. Bache Collection, 1949; pp. 34–35 Galleria dell'Accademia, Florence (Scala); p. 36 NYPL; p. 37 NYPL; p. 38 The Ashmolean Museum, Oxford; p. 39 Bulloz; p. 41 BM; p. 42 The Pierpont Morgan Library; p. 43 Schifanoia Palace, Ferrara (Scala); p. 45 Henry E. Huntington Library and Art Gallery; p. 46 Bulloz; p. 47 The Metropolitan Museum of Art, N.Y., Bequest of Maitland Fuller Griggs, 1943; p. 49 both NYPL; p. 50 S. Martino del Buonuomini, Florence (Scala); p. 53 Alte Pinakothek, Munich; p. 54 Kunsthistorisches Museum, Vienna (Photo Meyer Erwin); p. 57 Bibliothèque Nationale, Paris; p. 58 Yale University Library, Rare Books (Loebel); p. 59 Biblioteca Riccardiana, Florence (Scala); pp. 60–61 Bulloz; p. 62 Biblioteca Casanatense, Rome (Scala); p. 63 The Metropolitan Museum of Art, N.Y., the Cloisters Collection, Gift of John D. Rockefeller, Jr., 1937; p. 64 Palazzo Borromeo, Milan (Scala); p. 65 Time/Life; pp. 66–67 Kunsthistorisches Museum, Vienna (Photo Meyer Erwin); p. 70 Palazzo Vecchio, Florence (Scala); p. 73 BM; p. 75 The Metropolitan Museum of Art, N.Y. (Photo by Frank Lerner); p. 76 Christ Church, Oxford; p. 77 Hallwylska Museum, Stockholm; p. 78 BM; p. 79 Photographie Giraudon; p. 80 Bulloz; p. 81 (left) Archaeological Museum, Venice, (right) Frick Art Reference Library; p. 82 Biblioteca Communale, Forli (Scala); p. 83 Bulloz; p. 85 Bulloz; p. 86 Biblioteca Casanatense, Rome (Scala); p. 87 Biblioteca Riccardiana, Florence (Scala); p. 88 Photographie Giraudon; p.89 (left) BM, (right) Staatsbibliothek Berlin, Bildarchiv (Handke); p. 90 The Louvre, Paris; p. 93 Biblioteca Trivulziana, Milan (Scala); p. 95 Biblioteca Trivulziana, Milan (Scala); p. 96 Oespedale di Santi Spirito, Rome (Anderson-Alinari); p. 97 (top) The Metropolitan Museum of Art, N.Y., Rogus Fund, 1919; p. 99 Scala; p. 100 Staatsbibliothek, Berlin; p. 103 Palazzo Vecchio, Florence (Scala); p. 104 Galleria Borghese, Rome (Alinari); p. 105 The Metropolitan Museum of Art, N.Y., Harry Brisbane Dick Fund, 1938; p. 106 Museo di San Marco, Florence (Scala); p. 109 Pinacoteca Vanucci, Perugia (Alinari); p. 111 Nationalmuseum, Copenhagen; p. 115 Victoria & Albert Museum (Art-Wood Photography); p. 116 The Metropolitan Museum of Art, N.Y., Harris Brisbane Dick Fund, 1953; p. 117 Bibliothek Van de Rijksuniversiteit, Ghent; p. 119 Vatican, Rome (Scala); p. 120 Bibliotheque Royale de Belgique; p. 121 Church of San Michele (Alinari); p. 122 National Gallery, London; p. 125 Nationalbibliothek, Vienna; pp. 126–127 National Gallery, London; p. 128 NYPL; p. 129 The Metropolitan Museum of Art, N.Y., Gift of William H. Riggs, 1913; p. 130 Archivio di Stato, Siena (Alinari); p. 131 Alte Pinakotek, Munich; p. 132 (top) Metropolitan Museum of Art, N.Y., Fletcher Fund, 1929, (bottom) The Metropolitan Museum of Art, N.Y., Gift of William H. Riggs, 1913; p. 133 NYPL; p. 134 Palazzo Pubblico, Siena (Scala); p. 135 Galleria Nazionale Delle Marche, Urbino (Scala); pp. 136–137 BM; p. 140 Pinacoteca Vanucci, Perugia (Alinari); p. 141 Bruckmann-Art Reference Bureau; p. 143 The National Gallery, London; p. 145 S. Martino del Buonuomini, Florence (Scala); p. 147 Time/Life; p. 149 The Metropolitan Museum of Art, N.Y., Harris Brisbane Dick Fund, 1934; p. 151 The National Gallery, London; p. 152 from *Discovery and Exploration*, Geographical Projects; p. 153 Musées Royaux des Beaux-Arts, Brussels.

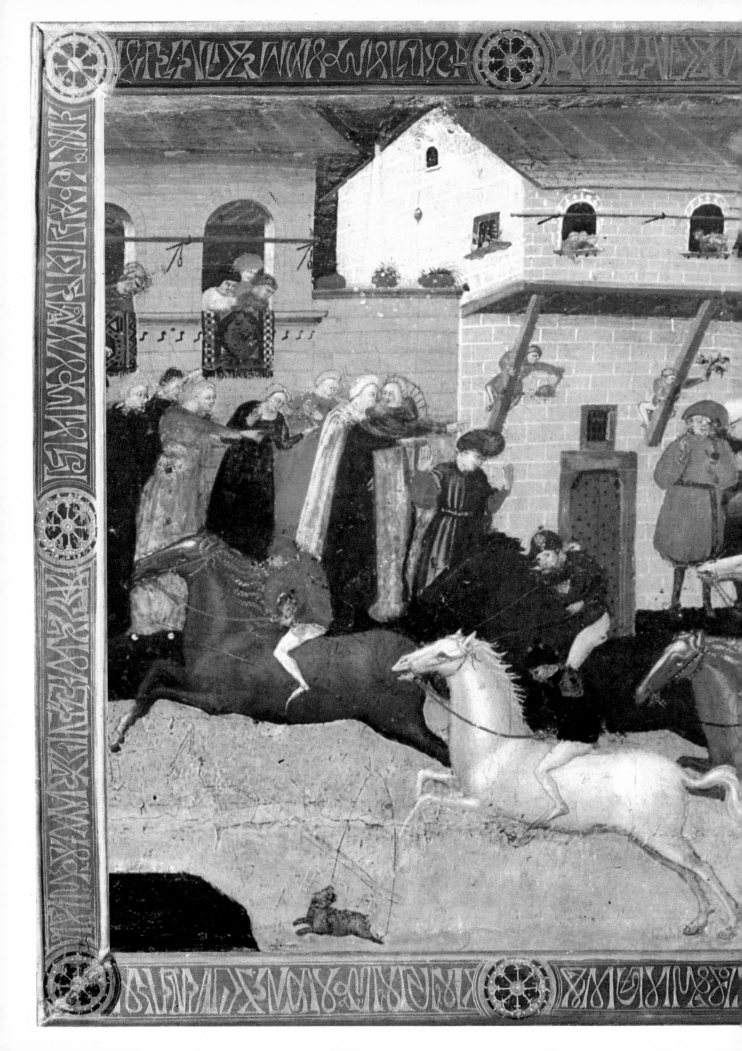